Assessing Children's Language

Assessing Children's Language
Guidelines for Teachers

Andrew Stibbs

Ward Lock Educational
in association with
The National Association for the Teaching of English

ISBN 0 7062 3853 2

First published 1979
Reprinted 1980

Set in 11 on 13 point Baskerville by Jubal Multiwrite Ltd, London SE13
and printed by Hollen Street Press Ltd at Slough, Berkshire
for Ward Lock Educational
116 Baker Street, London W1M 2BB
A member of the Pentos Group
Made in England

Contents

CHAPTER FOUR: 66
WHAT TO DO IN PRACTICE

Preface

This book is for teachers. In it we attempt to suggest some approaches to assessing children's language, to describe some practices, and to advise on some of the problems. We suggest that the most effective assessments of children's language are made by knowledgeable and sensitive teachers as part of their teaching. Other assessments may seem easier or more objective, but they are not necessarily more informative or useful.

At a time of cultural insecurity, there is a special unease about language, because language reflects social values. There are pressures on teachers — often from those least informed about language and education — to teach a narrow set of language skills and uses, and to accept 'teacher-free' assessments which seem to measure, more accurately than teachers can, the performances of children and schools.

We suggest that yielding to these pressures can often produce trivial, even misleading results, and can restrict or inhibit good classroom practice. In order to withstand these pressures teachers must be well informed. We hope that this book will be of some help to those who wish to think more about how to assess the language of the children they teach.

The book was produced by a working party of the North-East and Cleveland Durham Branches of the National Association for the Teaching of English. Bill Mittins was the chairman, and other members were Winifred Fawcus, Arthur Brookes, Gordon Hodgeon, Richard Nicholson, and Andrew Stibbs. They were helped by discussions with Pat D'Arcy, Pat Barrett, George Gyte, Mike Raleigh, and Mike Torbe. Others who gave advice on the text were Margaret Bond, John Dixon, Harold Gardiner, Colin Harrison, Pat Jones, Martyn Richards, and Alice Wakefield.

Many NATE members provided material for discussion, and we are grateful to them, and especially to the following individuals and schools for permission to describe their work, or use their materials:

Sheraton School, Cleveland
Pam Barnard, Dunstan Upper School, Northampton
Margaret Bond and Kate Coulter, Warsett School, Cleveland
Mervyn Riches, Woodway Park Comprehensive School, Coventry.

The text was written by Andrew Stibbs, with help from Mike Torbe and Leslie Stratta.

Chapter One:
When we are Assessing
– Four Illustrations

1 Looking at a piece of writing

One of our pupils is writing a story. She seems happy for us to watch over her shoulder. Sometimes she sucks her pen and looks out of the window. Sometimes she nudges her neighbour to ask or show her something. Should we leave her to it, or ask her how she's getting on? Sometimes as we pass she asks us a spelling. Should we tell her it? Here is the story she wrote:

'The day I teached (tort) the teachers

On day When I went up to the English Department all the teacher were sitting asait there, waiting for me to teach them. I dident now what to do so I gave them some books to read thay all read very good so I gave them all a A+ for it then I tooled them to write a story then Just as. they were going to write. then MR Cowdry came in I ask him why he was late he tooled me so I made him read a book I thought he was so good I gave him a A+ then they all should me they were (it was) so good I took them (it) to the head marster he said "there all good give em all a b+ for it" so I did but just as the bell went I woke up It was all a dream but I wished it was true.'

The original is hard to read because the setting-out is untidy. But we are practised in reading her work, and we can hear her reading it to us in our mind's ear. We enjoy the story, though we are disconcerted by the attitudes to assessment it displays, for which we feel partly responsible.

Now we get our red pen out and read it through again. Should we put marks on the page, or is this pupil one who regards marking as a defacement of her work rather than as a sign of our concern? Are we going to put full stops in? What about the spelling? Some words are spelt wrongly, but we know what they mean. Should we point out the mistakes, ask her to check them, correct them, or put a cross by them? What message would the writer understand by such markings? What about the correct spellings she got from us or her neighbour? What about where she crossed out 'teached' and wrote in 'tort'? Is that a plus or a minus? What about 'thay'? She spelt it wrongly first time but correctly the second. What about the ending? That sounds like a cliché to us, but what is it to her? Cliché, ingenuity, or a means of protecting herself? By whose standards should it be judged?

Now for a comment at the end. Should this refer to the content of her writing ('Have you often wished . . . ?') to our response as readers ('I found this enjoyable but hard to read . . . ') to our response as examiners ('Far too many spelling errors . . . ') or to what she should do next ('Write it out neatly . . . ' or 'How about reading this to the class?').

Suppose the writer is with us as we read the story. Should she read it to us or watch us reading it? If she watches, will we make noises such as tut-tutting the spellings or cheering the felicities? What are we going to do with the story? Keep it? Give it back? Show it to others? Shall we suggest a story like it for the writer to read? Shall we talk about our own attitudes to teaching and assessment? Shall we offer to type out the story or put it on the wall, or suggest that the writer puts it in a collection of her best stories? Shall we ask the writer how she wants her writing to be followed up?

What should we record in our mark book? The faulty spelling, the enjoyable overall effect, the help she sought from us and her neighbour, the apparent over-concern with grades, the way it is to be followed up, or a comparison with other stories by the writer?

Suppose we decide to give it a score. Will that be for the concentration that went into the writing, or for the effect of the story on us, or for the handwriting? What about 'tort'? Is that one on for 'grammar' or one off for mis-spelling? Suppose it's one off. Then how many off for each missing full stop? Which is most important? What about length? If we are 'knocking-off' markers, the longer the story the more marks we knock off; but should we give fewer marks for this story than we did to a shorter one which was less interesting? Suppose our score or grade is given 'on impression', so that length is rewarded. How do we decide the grade? By comparison with the writer's last piece, with the rest of the pieces from the class, with a national norm, with professional stories, or with perfection?

Every day we answer most of these questions. To do so, we refer to a stock of theoretical knowledge, or prejudice, previous experience, personal criteria and values, and our sense of pressures from children, the educational system and society. And those are not all the questions we answer. We answered some, for instance, when we decided it was all right to set a story or allow one to be written. Answering such questions, thinkingly or unthinkingly, is in fact assessing. In this sense we assess when we set, hear, or watch reading, when we set exercises or tests, and when we talk to children or talk to colleagues about them.

2 Administering a reading test

Now suppose we are testing a pupil's reading. Suppose we are using what is probably still the most widely used reading test in schools, Schonell's Graded Word Test ('tree; little; milk; egg . . . '). As the pupil reads the words aloud, we count the 'mistakes' he makes until we reach the point when we stop him and calculate his 'reading age'. What have we counted as a mistake? A hesitation followed by a correct pronunciation which might be a guess? A mispronunciation which may have been caused by a speech (not reading) defect, by a regional accent, or by using English as a second language? What about correct pronunciation of words we suspect the pupil does not know the meaning of? Suppose he does not know the meaning of the word in the isolation of the test. Might he not have been able to infer it correctly if he had met it in the context of continuous prose? In that case he might even have recognized it as a word he had heard, and pronounced it correctly. Should we allow for the age of the test, and discount the mispronunciation of 'canary', a word which occurs earlier in the test than the now-more-familiar 'university'?

Suppose we can answer or ignore all these questions, and administer the test with confidence. What has been tested or measured? It is reading, but reading of single words out of context. The words have no situation which could define their register and meaning. They have no visual illustrations (like those in most reading-scheme books) to indicate what they may denote. They do not even have surrounding sentences to give clues to their meanings and help them to be recognized. Is uncontextualized word recognition the sort of reading we really want to assess? If not, can we be sure that success at reading of this kind – at recognizing isolated words – correlates with success at 'real' reading? Are those pupils who are good at recognizing printed words by their shapes, or working out their sounds phonically, necessarily those who can read texts with most understanding, speed, or sensitivity? To read with understanding requires skills beyond word-recognition and phonic recoding.

The evidence we are using to assess even word-recognition is that of reading aloud to us. Could this evidence include factors which have nothing to do with 'real' reading, and which do not correlate with any reading abilities? Perhaps the child is shy, frightened, tired, or confused. Perhaps his difficulties are not so much in decoding print into meaning, as in recoding meaning into sound. Perhaps, in contrast, he is self-confident, motivated by the challenge to impress the teacher. Perhaps he has done the test before and has a good memory. Perhaps he has overheard other children in the group reading the word list.

So, even if we are confident that we have correctly judged which words the child has 'read', we cannot be sure that his performance is an accurate reflection of the ability to read in context, and with understanding. Our classroom organization, the way the test is administered, our mood, or the pupil's

4

mood or attitude may reduce the reliability of the test. Furthermore, are we sure that this test performance reflects the reading ability we are interested in? Is the result valid for the purpose for which we are going to use it?

The results of such reading tests are usually expressed as 'reading ages', equating a performance with that of an averagely-able child of that chronological age in the large sample on which the test was standardized. Test manuals point out the range of error of such results. Are we going to recognize that range of error in the way we express our results, or are we going to record our results in a way which seems to lend them an unjustifiable precision? Test manuals give the dates of standardizations of the tests. Are we aware of such dates? If we use out-of-date tests, our result may be depressed and give a false impression that standards are falling when they are not. This is because old tests are far more likely to include words (like 'canary') which have become less familiar and therefore harder to recognize with the passing of the years, than they are to include words which have become more familiar (or have been recently invented) and therefore more easily recognized since the test was last revised or standardized. The Schonell Graded Word Test was designed in the 1930s and re-standardized (with different results) in 1971 and 1973.

Finally, suppose we have a reading age for our pupil and we are aware of the limits of its reliability, its validity, and its comparability with national norms, how are we going to use the result? Perhaps we have an earlier score on this test for this pupil. If the latest score exceeds it by more than the increase of his chronological age since the last test, what shall we conclude from that? Perhaps the anomaly is within the range of error of the test. Perhaps it is because the earlier test was administered by a different teacher who interpreted the child's pronouncements in a different manner. Perhaps the pupil enjoyed the test more this time — especially if he remembered doing it before — and was less eager to escape anxiety by refusing each obstacle. Or perhaps we decide there really has been a significant improvement in his ability to recognize and pronounce words, beyond that which the increase in his age would predict. Are we therefore going to neglect his reading and give more attention to those who have made less progress? Are we going to recommend harder books to him, with no further check on his ability to understand them?

Suppose another pupil has improved less than we hoped. Is the poor progress to be explained as all that can be expected anyway from someone who scores below average in this test, or is it a danger signal? If it is a case of the latter, what remedial action does it suggest to us? Does it tell us why the pupil is making poor progress, or what his special difficulties are? Suppose the pupil's score is actually lower than in a previous test. Do we therefore believe that his reading ability has declined, or do we mistrust the test procedure?

Even when we use a standardized objective test we must still make many personal assessments, consciously or unconsciously. We must assess the reliability of our use of the test, the validity of the inferences we make from the results, and assessments of what to do with the results, and how to alter our teaching in their light.

3   Listening to a pupil read aloud

Supposing, however, that we are listening to the pupil's everyday reading, rather than testing it; many of the same questions will arise. If, for instance, a primary school pupil is reading to us from a book in a reading scheme, we again have evidence of problems of understanding mediated through reading aloud. We may also have some of the problems of the artificiality of the text, since some schemes, especially if they use careful gradations of words according to their phonetic simplicity or their frequency, may be only a little more related to the language the child knows than is the string of words in a word-recognition test. But in this case we have extra resources to aid our assessment. If the pupil is reading a book, he can give us more evidence of his reading strategies. We can see if he looks to illustrations, or to subsequent text, to help him work out a word he is unsure of. We can note whether his incorrect guesses would make sense or fit the syntax of the sentence. We can ask questions to check if he understands what he is reading. In so doing we may be teaching the reading we are assessing. To give a very simple example, to say 'Well what do you think the

6

word might be? Look at the picture', might teach the pupil to use context-clues, as well as giving him the confidence to guess.

In this situation we may also be given clearer hints about how to follow up our assessment. If the pupil is reading with complete ease, even boredom, we may decide to let him skip a step in his reading-scheme sequence. If he is reading fluently but still needing to work out some words, we may decide his ability and his reading material are properly matched. If he is struggling, we may decide to move him sideways onto a supplementary reader when he has finished this book. We may even decide to find an easier book. If he is reading quickly but carelessly, relying too much on such clues as pictures and too little on the print, we may seek out a book without illustrations for him next. If he is gabbling monotonously, we may ask him to read a page silently then tell us what it said in his own words. We may even decide he needs glasses.

Again, the process is continual. In this case it is obviously interwoven with teaching, diagnosis, and with planning future work for a pupil.

4   Responding to examination answers
For our last example of an everyday school situation, which raises many questions for the teacher about assessing children's language, let us imagine that the children in a secondary school have been answering an end-of-year English examination. They have been sitting in silence, working to a time-limit. They have had to write a continuous piece of prose chosen from a number of titles, and read a passage and answer comprehension questions about it.

All the examination scripts will be given a score by one teacher who may well grade the continuous writing on impression, and mark the comprehension exercise according to a marking scheme. (Some of the technical problems of such marking will be raised in the third chapter.) Some of the questions the marker will have to ask have already been raised; for instance how much to weight technical error or competence in comparison with originality or banality of style or content, or how best to judge language ability on such evidence as writing on an unchosen or unsuitable topic, or written answers to set questions on a passage read for no purpose beyond answering the questions on it.

We shall use this last illustration to raise just one set of further questions about assessment. These questions concern the effects of the activities which we promote (in this case pupils sitting the examination) to help us in our assessments, and whether or not one of those effects is to help them to learn. In sitting the examination the pupils will have done a fair amount of reading, writing, and, presumably, thinking. There has been a pressure on them to 'think on their feet' about topics they would not consider unless forced to do so by the examination. Examinations can be a stimulus for major, perhaps even permanent, advances in thought for some students, especially at sixth-form or college level. On the other hand, they take time out of teaching. Moreover, in examinations, pupils cannot seek the help of books, teachers, other pupils, or talk. They cannot let their developing interests power their language activities, or organize the time they spend on them. They may be anxious about their performances in the examination and the use to which the results will be put, and that anxiety may be reinforced by the solemn ritual with which examinations are accompanied. The anxiety may mar their performances so that their results are misleading indicators of their abilities under normal conditions. The anxiety may become associated with the activities of reading, writing, and thinking in general, so that future learning is made distasteful.

Sometimes pupils do not get back their examination scripts. Sometimes they get them back with nothing more than the mark which a teacher, perhaps not their own, has written on them. What do they learn from such marking about the purpose of writing, or how to do it better? What do we learn from examination scripts, or the grades our pupils earn? The grades may help us to predict performances in some external examinations, but do they help us to judge how each pupil should best be taught? Are they the most useful evidence to put in our record books? Are they the best guides to what parents reading the reports we write about their children want to know? Is what we, and what the pupils do with examination results a sufficient justification of the time, money, and distress which they may cost?

Summary

In these four illustrations we have tried to show some of the many questions about our pupils' language which are raised in our day-to-day teaching, and how we answer them, consciously, unconsciously, or by default, in assessing. Assessing is an everyday, continuing, conscious or unconscious part of teaching. For example, we show our assessment of a pupil's language when we smile at it, listen to it, or read it, especially if we read it aloud to a class. As we do those things we can reinforce its good qualities and stimulate our pupils to produce more.

If we are aware that in some way or other we are assessing a great deal of the time, we can control the effects of our assessing. These effects are an integral part of our teaching. That is why the question, 'How will this assessment help the pupil?' has become increasingly insistent throughout these introductory illustrations. We all have different experiences, values and interpretations of the demands made on us, so our assessments may not be uniform; but if we can clarify our assessing procedures, we can make them reasonable and responsible.

In this introductory chapter, we have raised some of the practical questions of assessment. In subsequent chapters we shall deal more systematically with the fundamental issues from which these questions arise, and the principles underlying methods of assessment.

Chapter Two:
What we are Assessing

We can organize the many random everyday questions of assessment such as those raised in the illustrations of the last chapter. Assessment of children's language will only be consistently helpful if it is based on some well-thought principles. Some of these principles are values, but they also need to be built upon some sort of structure, some assumptions about the nature of language and learning. This chapter will try to provide that structure.

SECTION 1:
THE SURFACE FEATURES OF LANGUAGE USE

The detailed surface features of language use are obvious. It is easy to judge when words are correctly recognized and pronounced. Handwriting is either immediately legible or it is not. The qualification of nouns with many adjectives may sometimes be a feature of precise and vivid writing which is easy to measure or even to quantify. We can even tell something of a person's origin by his accent without listening to what he says. But these surface features of language may mislead us about a person's use of language. We suggested in Chapter One some dangers in taking word-recognition as a guide to reading ability. Similarly, an ability to pronounce a word correctly does not prove an ability to use or understand it. Handwriting can sway our judgment of the message it conveys. We have all seen children's writing spoiled because they have mechanically qualified nouns with lots of adjectives, making what could have been an effective and direct statement into mannered 'fine writing'. We are misled by glib speakers, the superficial attractiveness of whose speech disguises their unattractive meanings.

It is tempting to base assessment of children's language on these surface features because they are easy to recognize and to agree on. If they become the only criteria used in assessment, assessment becomes a straightforward, non-controversial topic and something which, in theory, machines could perform.

If we examine the consequences of a limited view of assessment concentrating on surface features, its drawbacks may become obvious. We shall take a case history first, to discover what the limited view makes of assessment in one mode of language use.

Marking a story

For the case history, we return to continuous writing, since it is easy to present the evidence. Here is another story, written by an older pupil than the one who wrote the story in Chapter One. We set it out as it appeared after a teacher had marked it.

Lost in the Fog

The chilling night air felt dampening on my warm brow, I walked on past a what seemed to be a thousand acre field of under ripe beetroots. The evening mist began to fall, slowly at first, then before I knew it I was stranded, the place I knew not. My view was obscured by the dazzling on coming head lights The time was getting late, the exact time I could'nt tell for sure onething I knew was if the fog did'nt lift soon, that would be the end **what?** to my <u>late fridays.</u> I walked on, only to find myself lying flat out in the middle of a laural bush. At the time I

Re-read what you write to make it read sensibly

11

could'nt rememb~~er~~ what I had done, it
seem~~s~~ to all come back to me ~~know~~,
yes, A car, a Volo I think, came shooting
oup the road, I steped back and there I

*Avoid
slang*

was flat out. I must have triped oVer a
man hole cover or som~~thing~~, yes, ~~know~~
I can rem~~e~~mber putting my hand on some
thing cold, with little lumps on, It did'nt
occure to me at the time least ways until
I got home that I sat on something else
as well.

I stood up a little dazed reolised the

*Avoid these
Careless
errors*

time and ran. When I stopped I seemed to
be more lost than ever. I sat down

*were
where*

and tried to work it out, were I had come
from, and in what direction I was to head,
I had seen it done on the tele, everything vision

*find a
better word*

worked ~~great~~ and he found himself at home
eating dinner within ten minutes. It did'nt
work.

I decided I was getting no were fast.
I found that I was doing nothing only
getting ~~tiered~~. I walked a little longer,
I could see a light shin~~n~~ing through the
fog, I walked toward it. It was a laundrette,
lucky for me it was open. I walked in and
a little bell above the door rang, it stopped

so I shut the door. I did'nt recognise the surroundings but I was intending to get to know them, for a few hours any way.

There was know movement any whre, the familer rattling of the machines was gone. There were no noisy shoppers standing arround chattering as most shoppers do. The whole world felt dead. It was weared hearing nothing only my own heart beat, thump, thump.

I looked arround looking for the warmest part of the room, which I found to be next to the big heat driers. My fingers felt ~~went~~ numb. I rubed my hands together to warm them. My eye lids were getting heavy.

I must have dropped off I was awoken by a window cleaner who was cleaning the shop windows. I still in daylight could'nt recognised were I had landed my self. I stood up, from what I can remember, and stretched my legs. The window cleaner started to stare at me. I looked on the clock which I ~~hadent~~ noticed before it was half past nine. I stepped outside and took a deep breath of cold clean air.

The name of the street I was in was
called Middlefield Ave., then I knew that
I wasn't far away from home, it was only
ten minutes walk, so home I went.

Expecting only the worst. *Not a sentence*

(5/20) *Far too many careless errors of spelling and punctuation. You must keep closer to the essay title and write about the fog.*

The teacher has marked this story very conscientiously. In his comments, in the margin and at the end, his criticisms concentrate on four features — relevance to the title, spelling errors, punctuation errors, and style. Since it is not made clear how the story is irrelevant to the title, we shall look at how the other three features are marked.

The marker says the spelling errors are 'careless', as if the writer could have avoided all of them if he had written more slowly or perhaps gone over the piece afterwards. This may be true of many of the errors, though fast and excited writing may have produced the desirable vividness, which we would not want to sacrifice for perfect spelling. Perhaps the teacher had not allowed enough time for the pupil to check through after the writing, especially to check those words which the writer did not suspect were misspelt. 'Remember', for instance, is a word spelt incorrectly at first but correctly later. So the writer can spell 'remember' (or can bring his 'passive' memory of the word's spelling into his 'active' ability when he is sensitized by the excitement of being involved in his writing). If that is so, is there any point in the teacher correcting it, as distinct from pointing it out? However, 'dazzeling' may be a careful spelling. The word is not often seen and it is often pronounced in the way this spelling would suggest. A teacher who wanted the writer to learn the correct spelling would have to write it out. 'Know' is not a spelling error but the incorrect use of a correctly spelt word for its homonym. This may be the result of 'over-teaching' which confuses pupils into over-correcting all 'were's' into

14

'where's' and all plural s's into apostrophe s's. Elsewhere in the piece, 'knew' is spelt correctly.

What will be the effect of the teacher's corrections of misspelt words? Will the pupil make sure that he spells them correctly when he uses them in future? Or could it be that he will avoid using them, or similarly ambitious words? Some of the misspelt words, like 'dazzeling', may have been better accepted as they are (as is 'laural'), or even praised. In the marking of this piece there is no praise for the choice of words, only criticism for their spelling. Because correctness of spelling can often occupy an important place in the limited view of assessment, it has been applied in the marking of this piece with too little discrimination. The corrections do not take sufficient account of the reasons for the different spelling errors (carelessness is only one reason), and the effects of correcting so many of them.

There is, however, less marking of the punctuation by the teacher. The way 'could'nt' is corrected is helpful teaching rather than criticism. However, even on a limited view of assessment, it seems a relatively trivial mistake to denote time to, with a writer who seems to need more help with handwriting and spelling.

The comment 'not a sentence' on 'Expekting only the worst' is an example of how a limited understanding of language can mislead. Out of context, the words are not a sentence, and their use like this is a stylistic error. But in the context of a colloquial story, they are a complete, meaningful unit, and one whose meaningfulness is enhanced by its very 'ungrammatical' brevity. If the marking of the story had been informed by a wider view of assessment, which took into account some of the less obvious features of the language, some of the faults of the story (such as the carelessness), may have been treated as a price worth paying for some of its virtues such as fluency. Some might even have been seen as virtues in themselves. The 'incorrect' grammar of this last sentence, 'Expekting only the worst', is such an example: it contributes to the appropriate tone. Another is the 'slang', which the marker tells the writer to avoid, but which is essential to the feeling and subject matter of the story.

Tone (which conveys the writer's attitude to the reader) and feeling (which conveys his attitude to his subject matter) are examples of the good qualities in the story, which a more complex view of language and its assessment might have led the marker to recognize. Another is the shaping of the narrative so that the reader is involved. This is not a measurable quality, like some of the obvious surface features of language, but it is one whose importance we implicitly acknowledge whenever we feel sufficiently involved with a story or novel to want to read on. The opening of 'Lost in the Fog' creates an eerie mood and an anticipation of events to come. It uses vague words and phrases like 'seemed', 'before I knew', 'obscured', 'knew not', and 'couldn't tell for sure', which help the reader to share the narrator's disorientation. The uncanny stillness of the launderette is dramatically extended, and described in words which are well chosen (but earn only four 'sp's as marked). The ending secures the story in the reader's imagination by creating an anticipation the reader must fulfil himself.

A teacher with a more complex understanding of language and learning and its assessment would praise features such as these, as well as selectively correcting spelling, thereby encouraging the writer to write more and develop his strengths. If the piece had been graded with this approach to assessment, such features would earn marks at least as quickly as spelling errors lost them. How helpful is the mark '5/20', when it is not explained what the five marks were gained for and the fifteen lost for, nor how the writer could improve his writing sufficiently to earn '6/20' or '20/20'? To conclude, the teacher has focused his whole attention on observable surface features which he assesses as right or wrong; and on the basis of those has come to an assessment of the qualities of the whole piece.

Assessing reading

For a comparison of how a narrow or complex view of language would assess another mode of language use we shall take reading. We do this because two of the illustrations in Chapter One will provide some support for these more general remarks and because far more is known about the processes of reading than the processes of writing or talk.

In the first chapter we referred loosely to 'reading ability',

16

and we shall say more about abilities later in this chapter. If we attempt to make a crude list of elements in reading ability, and list them in a roughly hierarchical way, they might look like this:

1 *Knowing the print conventions of language*
  In English we write and read from left to right and from top to bottom, and separate words by blank spaces.
2 *Associating printed symbols with sounds*
  In the case of words, there is a one-to-one correspondence, but it is more complicated in the case of letters or letter-groups, where twenty-six letters must represent forty-five sounds in English.
3 *Recognizing the concepts or experiences denoted by separate words*
  There are the 'dictionary definitions' which limit the use of words to certain meanings without precisely defining their actual uses and meanings in contexts.
4 *Comprehending the meanings of words in immediate contexts*
  These are more exact meanings which depend on their immediate contexts but may alter in different contexts. They are, however, related to each other and to their 'dictionary meanings'. To illustrate how a word has its meaning sharpened by its immediate context, think of how 'deep' near the end of 'Lost in the Fog' is given precision by its association with 'breath'.
5 *Making meaning in a wider context*
  This is the ability to see how the meanings of sentences and paragraphs relate to each other and modify each other. This ability is essential in order to appreciate how an argument develops, or narrated events form a sequence, or images are patterned in a poem, or how a text has to be read selectively for a particular purpose. To illustrate how the meaning of a passage takes on greater resonance, think of how the meaning of 'Lost in the Fog' is being progressively modified as we read this booklet, by our concern for, and understanding of, assessment.

17

6 *Responding personally to a text*

In any response, the reader brings prior experience, interests, and purposes to the text, so that the text is re-shaped in forms which can be built on to what the reader brings to the text. Equally the text can modify the reader's experience, interests, and purposes, leading him to immediate action or long-term change. It is a particular interaction unique to each reading. Consider, for example, reading a practical book, such as a gardening manual, where the interaction between reading and experience can enable the reader to engage with the information being offered, and, at the same time, to adopt new practices.

The Bullock Report, *A Language for Life*, (17.6 page 251) showed how widely such tests as we described in our second illustration of Chapter One are used. Most standardized tests of reading take the first of the above elements in reading ability for granted, and concentrate on testing elements 2, 3, and sometimes, 4. Many, like the Schonell Word-Recognition Test (published by Oliver and Boyd) are restricted to elements 2 and, possibly, 3. Some, like the Holborn Reading Scale, (published by Harrap) may test element 4 as well, because the words to be recognized and read aloud are arranged in sentences which provide contexts that aid the recognition of unfamiliar words. Other tests, where missing words can only be inferred from their contexts, also test element 4. Examples of these are tests which leave words out, such as the GAP test (published by Heinemann), or which leave sentences to be completed, such as the Wide Span Test (Nelson), or offer multiple choice of words from which to select a gap-filler, such as the Watts-Vernon test. It is true that there are reading tests which use continuous passages of prose, such as the Neale Analysis (published by Macmillan) or the Schonell Silent Reading Tests (published by Oliver and Boyd) but, as we shall argue later, asking questions about continuous passages does not necessarily test 'making meaning in a wider context', or even recognizing dictionary meanings. It depends on the questions. There are ways of assessing reading which take elements 5 and 6 into account, as will be argued in the next chapter, but not by using existing standardized tests.

Of course, if we use standardized tests, it does not necessarily mean that we think reading is limited to only the first three or four elements, but there is a danger that the prestige and apparent objectivity which tests possess will give the impression that those elements are the most important. For instance, teaching children to read with a reading scheme, as in our third illustration of Chapter One, may concentrate our attention on checking the pupil's recognition and pronunciation of words, to the exclusion of checking his understanding of them. The 'early' elements are essential to reading, but reading which includes elements 5 and 6 goes on developing in schools from an early stage and needs to be actively encouraged. It also should be recognized in the assessment of reading. A narrow view of assessment may limit both assessing and teaching to the first three or four elements, thus transforming reading into an impersonal, ineffective, and trivial process, which never reaches the stage where the reader and the meaning of the text interact profitably.

That trivializing effect of a narrow view of assessment is one which also applies to other modes. To be a good proof-reader (an expert in the 'early' elements) a reader has to ignore meaning, whereas a good reader (an expert in all elements) looks for meaning. He may not even notice the superficial: efficient readers often overlook misprints, and if we are bilingual we can read bilingual texts without noticing which parts are in which language. So with the marking of 'Lost in the Fog', a concentration on proof-reading (informed by a limited view of assessment) deflected attention from reading for meaning. To be a good proof-writer, a writer may have to concentrate on the superficial features of his writing to the exclusion of meaning. Think how we are liable to make absurd mistakes when we do decorative lettering. And in the mode of talking, we might consider it best to train and to test clarity of pronunciation, for instance, with nonsense-sentences such as 'How now, brown cow'. But that would be to do a disservice to talking.

SECTION 2:
LANGUAGE AS A PROCESS

We have been talking of the surface features of language. The Bullock Report says (1.10): 'Language competence grows incrementally through an interaction of writing, talking, reading and experience, the body of resulting work forming an organic whole.' We have quoted this for two reasons. First, it emphasizes the coherence and interrelationship of different language modes, something which will be assumed in this section, but which a concentration on surface features of language may ignore. Second, it introduces the metaphor of a body, for language competence. This is an instructive metaphor. It emphasizes that language grows. An individual child's language competence grows all the time, sometimes inevitably, sometimes only with help, sometimes quickly, sometimes not. In general, language evolves, so that to expect it to remain the same is misguided. The metaphor also keeps the word 'diagnosis' before our attention: a teacher, like a doctor, should seek the causes of problems, not just recognize that problems exist.

To pick up the theme of the last section, the metaphor reminds us that what appears on the surface of language is symptomatic of deeper and more vital strengths and weaknesses. The limited view of language treats symptoms instead of causes. In practice, we often have to study, teach and assess the *processes* of language through its *products*. This happens for example, when we read what a child has written after the event. Many of the most important language uses are not susceptible to direct investigation. Thought, for example, is a process we cannot easily examine directly. Sometimes it is a process accompanied by expression and communication. Where this happens the thinking processes result in a language product — a recorded utterance, a written note, a printed poem, a completed essay, or a filled gap in an exercise. In these cases we have evidence to work on. We can use the surface features to approach the underlying thought, even though it is not the surface features in which we are principally interested. *How* the thought is communicated is important: if the letter is illegible or the speech incomprehensible, the communication fails. But *what* is communicated is equally, if not more important and we should be keen to understand and develop that.

It is comparatively easy to judge and to correct the means and manners of communication. The success of the manner will be embodied in such tangible evidence as correct spelling. That is why it is understandable that when we are tired we correct a pupil's written work without reading what it is telling us. It is why employers and parents focus their unease about language upon such obvious features as spelling, handwriting, and articulation. It is why talking is often valued less than the more tangible writing. It is much harder to assess the qualities of the thought processes which have generated language. Often the external appearance of language does not truly reflect the depth of a pupil's thought. As teachers, we have to use our imaginations and personal judgments, and not limited yardsticks, to discern the quality of thinking behind what a pupil says or writes. If we omit to do this, and concentrate instead only on the means and manners, we fail to develop and assess the important language processes, without which the products of language are trivial. The view of language, suggested in the previous section, recognizes the importance of process in language and tries to take it into account in assessments, by looking for the meaning behind the manner, and by diagnosing the causes of the surface blemishes.

A practical aid to assessing language processes as well as products might be expressed thus: try to get as near as possible to the place and time of the language process. In general, we will have more understanding of a pupil's writing, and be able to offer more help with the difficult process, if we are available to him as he writes. Had we been present when 'Lost in the Fog' was written, we might have been able to answer some of those questions which we raised when we looked at the finished product. To listen to a pupil read, and watch him, and perhaps discuss his reading with him, is a better aid to understanding his reading processes and his problems, than to study his written answers to questions about a text. If we are with the reader we can see his hesitations, skippings, backtrackings and guessings, and learn from them. To have a conversation with a pupil may

21

tell us more about how he copes with a conversation than to listen to a tape-recording of his speech. To hear pupils talking about the books they are in the process of reading can often help us to assess their responses whereas reviews written after reading may not necessarily reveal how some pupils have responded.

Here are two extreme but instructive examples of the consequences of treating language as a process rather than a product. Note-taking and note-making are two language processes which pupils in secondary, further, and higher education use. Teachers complain that pupils do not take or make notes well. Yet the processes are rarely taught. Could this be because the products of these processes, the pupils' notes, are traditionally none of the teacher's concern? Is it because the products are thought unimportant, that the process is ignored? But if we take a complex view of language the process of thoughtful listening or reading, which is aided by taking notes, is a very important one. So is the organization of original thought, a process which uses the making of one's own notes.

The second example of the consequences of regarding language as process is that mistakes in the surface features of children's language can not only be seen to have different causes and different levels of importance, but they may even, in some cases, be evidence of progress, of difficulties overcome, as well as difficulties still to be overcome. If our preschool children have the words 'fed' and 'mice' amongst the first words they learn, it is probable that there will come a time in their third year of life when they begin to say 'feeded' and 'mouses'. This is because they have begun to infer some of the general rules of grammar (to put a word into the past you add 'ed' to it, and to make a word plural you add 's' to it). Children, on the whole, apply the rules regularly at first. In this case the logical application of the rules leads to a 'mistake', because some words are irregular in their morphology. Thus, on the surface, the correctness of 'fed' and 'mice' has been succeeded by the incorrectness of 'feeded' and 'mouses'. However, an understanding of language acquisition recognizes this as a step forward, not backward, because it is a symptom of a new power to generate many more sentences and meanings (most of which will be correct in their surface grammar) by applying these newly-learnt rules to the words which the child already knows.

When a child learns to read, he first learns to sound out the words separately. As his fluency grows, and his familiarity with sequences of words and their connections with messages increases, he will begin to guess words from their first letters or rough outlines, then from their contexts only, skipping some altogether. When a child has the confidence to do this he will probably also make some mistakes: the wrong word may be a guess. But if the guessed word could fit the context, we may count it not so much as a mistake as a sign of improved reading technique, and a step on the road to becoming a reader with a variety of reading styles for different purposes, including the ability to read quickly or scan. In our analysis of 'Lost in the Fog' we suggested how some mistakes (like misspelt ambitious words) might be welcomed for what they indicated. Emotional involvement, or grappling with difficult ideas, can be causes of mistakes in written work just as much as carelessness or ignorance. Similarly, if a pupil 'loses himself' in a complicated spoken utterance, we may welcome the intention shown by the attempt, rather than condemn the incompetence shown by the failure. A pupil makes progress in his language development by struggling at the frontier of his knowledge and competence.

There are obvious teaching implications in this second extreme example of the consequences of a more complex view of language and assessment. Mistakes may be tolerated which, in a narrow view, would not be. Attention may not be drawn to them, lest the pupil fixes his attention on the surface features of the language products rather than on the underlying process. The decorative letterer who makes spelling mistakes is disabled by his over-concentration on surface features. A learner of a language, native or foreign, may be thrown by being asked to read aloud a text that he is beginning to make sense of through reading silently. It is like asking a pianist to think about his fingers.

SECTION 3:
'THE BASICS'

The narrow view of 'basics'

If the assessment of children's language is not to trivialize language teaching, it will be concerned with the most important features of the language process. What are these features which belong to the narrow and the more complex views of language and its assessment?

In our rough hierarchy of elements relating to the ability to read, the early ones — those which standardized tests assess — are clearly 'basic' in the sense that they are essential before a reader can begin to read. A pupil cannot make a worthwhile personal response to a book if he cannot recognize the words it is written in. Similarly, writing which is illegible, or talk which is inaudible, are worthless as forms of communication, though they might be parts of worthwhile thought processes.

Although they are *necessary* conditions of reading well, those early elements are not *sufficient* in themselves to bring about the ability to read well. As we have suggested, a level of reading which merely recognizes the conventions of print, pronounces it correctly, and even recognizes the dictionary meaning of each word, is not good reading. It makes no meaning of, and has no uses for, the whole text. Thus if we treat only the obvious elements of reading ability as 'basic', we may neglect, in teaching and assessing, the more complex and less tangible processes which give reading its worth.

In later sections we shall suggest, as we have hinted at the end of the last section, that by concentrating only on the obvious, we may actually hold children back. For the moment, let us refer to the marking of 'Lost in the Fog' for the effect of a limited view of 'the basics' . The teacher's concentration on what are popularly considered the 'basics' of writing (correct spelling, conventional punctuation, Standard English grammar, and polite vocabulary) has caused him to neglect equally important features such as tone, form, and realistic detail, as we have suggested. Sometimes the popular view of basics may conflict with our estimation of what are important features of successful

24

writing, such as whether polite vocabulary is more important than tone. It is debatable just how basic some of the 'basics' are, especially in writing. For example, because they have such a variety of causes, not all spelling mistakes are equally important, especially when one considers language as a process and mistakes as evidence of this process. In the great majority of cases perfect spelling is not essential to making meaning. Of course, conventional spelling makes a text *easier* to read, and we would not want to undervalue its importance, but if spelling mistakes were really a barrier to a reader's understanding these spellings would not be recognized as mistakes but taken to be unfamiliar and incomprehensible words. (This example suggests why an ability to recognize *every* word is not basic to reading.) Similarly, most correct punctuation is an aid, rather than a necessity, to understanding. Only a small proportion is 'basic', namely those mistakes in punctuation which make part of a text unintelligible or ambiguous.

A complex view of basics

What would we add to the popular list of basics? If one thinks of language, and how human beings use it, there are few simple neat lists of features of successful uses of language. Some obviously distinct and recognizable features are spelling, word-recognition, or intelligibility to a listener with Received Pronunciation. However, because many features of successful uses of language are not neatly classifiable, they are in danger of being neglected when there is a demand for objective assessment, especially because these features are felt to be unnecessary if the teacher merely pays attention to spelling and punctuation. What further concerns are fundamental to successful uses of language, and ought to be recognized in assessment? We will describe three.

1   *Meaning*

One of our basics which has already been mentioned is meaning. There is a problem — too wide-ranging to be dealt with in this book — of how we should regard and assess language which conveys meanings which engage our personal, political, ethical or spiritual values so strongly that we feel that our valuing it as language is irrelevant. It is raised, for example, by the values inherent in a work of literature which clash with those of the reader.

In a different context it can be raised by our pupils in the effective expression of offensive opinions. Most of us would feel we have no right to impose our own views on pupils, nor to protect them from views we dislike. But we might stress that we value the meaningfulness of language and the skill in clearly detecting the meanings which others convey (by recognizing and evaluating propaganda and rhetoric, for instance). Teachers with a care for meaning will want pupils to use language to live and think with, to be direct and not merely decorative in their speech and writing, to grapple with difficult ideas, even at the cost of clumsy language, to be able to put aside the distractions of spelling mistakes, or of different regional accents or social class in evaluating what they read or hear.

2 Care

The word 'care' in 'care for meaning' is as basic as meaning. In its sense of 'caring', and in its sense of 'careful', care is a basic of language use. Without a commitment to the meaning he intends to convey, a language user might be described as 'glib', 'hypocritical', or 'mechanical' — words which carry pejorative connotions, whatever our political, ethical, or spiritual values. A care to find or make meaning — ('motivation') — amplifies ability in the use of language, as we shall try to illustrate later. The desire to find out what a text has to say makes readers more successful, which is why young football fans often make more sense of the morning paper than of their carefully graded school reading schemes, and why children seem to have higher 'reading ages' in subjects they like at school than in subjects they dislike. (This could be demonstrated by comparing the 'readability indices' of the texts which they understand in the respective subjects.) The careful attention which commitment to written work brings is revealed by the way the spelling improved in the writing of the two stories we have quoted, the writing of which was clearly enjoyed by the writers. The incentive of having a real readership or purpose for written work, or a real felt need for its correctness, may produce careful attitudes and an attempt to achieve correctness in pupil writers which conventional marking would not. They will proof-read work which is to go to the school secretary for typing, look up words they are going to use in the school magazine, and fair-copy work for display on the walls. It has to be emphasized, though, that in some circumstances, this 'care' may well result in speed rather than laboriousness, in directness rather than elaboration, and in the taking of risks as well as fastidiousness.

3   Imaginative Abilities

We can list some basic abilities too, as long as we stress that they may be skills which may not be so easily isolated as those in conventional lists, such as handwriting. It is clear how meaningful language content, care in the attitude of the language-user, and language ability interact, from the example we gave of the effect of care on performance. Care amplifies skill. Skill can encourage the taking of more care. Both increase meaning. A sense of having a meaning to convey produces care. And so on. In the elements of reading listed earlier, abilities clearly play a part in the early ones, such as knowledge of conventions, sign/ sound relationships, and dictionary meanings, and the habit of using an immediate context to define the meanings of words. In the fifth and sixth element an ability to relate is important. In element 5, the reader uses an ability to relate possibilities of the text to his own experiences and intentions, and in element 6, he uses an ability to relate parts to the whole.

That ability to relate depends a good deal on experience of the varieties of language use and upon the exercise of imagination. A sense of variety and imagination are also basics of language use. The former consists of realizing that there are varieties of tones and registers in language, and of realizing which are appropriate for different modes (such as speaking or writing) and different styles related to different social contexts (such as playgrounds or classrooms), different audiences (such as sweethearts or magistrates) and different purposes (such as informing or persuading). To be versatile in the use of language is as important as being correct in language form. A sense of appropriateness may even override notions of correctness. In some contexts the seemingly incorrect may be appropriate, and therefore, to most of us, preferable. (For example, colloquial and elliptical uses of language such as: 'Don't try to chat me up. It won't work', can be very appropriate.)

To apply such versatility aptly, and to make the sorts of relationships that element six requires, a language user needs empathy and imagination, our third example of a basic ability. Imagination is basic not just to the bizarre fancy of the easiest kinds of 'creative' writing, but to everyday language uses. Even to write or react to warnings needs a power to imagine you are someone else at another time or in another place, with different preconceptions and concerns. To use language effectively, a language user needs to imagine the producer's intentions or the receiver's response. That sympathetic power is one which employers require. They want apprentices who can interpret instructions or report machine faults to those who don't have the physical evidence of the machine before them. They want shopgirls who can talk to customers without unintentionally giving offence. The basic imagination to do this may best be developed not by unreal exercises, but by literature, drama, realistic simulations and creative writing. Such implications will be developed further in the next section.

SECTION 4:
IMPLICATIONS FOR TEACHING

What are the practical implications of a view of language in which the basics include meaningfulness, care and imaginative abilities?

We have already suggested that our concern for language will be a concern for meaning and for the truth and values of what is meant. We will not, in our teaching, want to encourage 'language for language's sake'.

If language is to be a skilful making of meaning, its makers must care about it, and use it for reasons which seem good to them. These reasons may not include to 'learn English'. Paradoxically, the best English teaching is not always done by teaching English directly. It may be done by encouraging something else which requires English. Teaching 'the basics' may be accomplished by valuing and developing incidental talk, by exploiting unexpected opportunities for pupils to write, and finding reasons for them to read. All these teaching and learning occasions crop up in all classrooms as part of the natural relationships between pupils and pupils, and between pupils and teachers. They require the teacher to be willing to set aside time for open-ended individual work, if they are to be properly used. But to do this well teachers need to have a sophisticated and not a narrow understanding of language, and how human beings use it.

Finally, the traditional 'basics' — which we want to develop but not to the detriment of other important aspects of language use — will be strengthened when they are seen by pupils to have a purpose. Where a pupil has a meaning to make, and cares about making it, he will want to be able to master the conventions of language, without which his tongue, pen, or eyes will do less than justice to his intentions. The niceties of language will become instances of a worthy respect for the reader, listener, or writer of words the pupil works with. When he feels he needs these abilities, he is more likely to learn them fairly easily. The activities which best practise and develop these basics, as well as those we have added, are not necessarily the most formal and utilitarian. They will include imaginative work pursued for its own sake in the self-initiated pupil activities which often elicit their greatest efforts in language.

We show below three examples of language-learning experiences in schools by adolescents classified as below average at English, with teachers alert to the possibilities which can arise. They illustrate this section, and the next, because they suggest implications for assessment of children's language. In each, there is a pressure on the pupil to make meaning, which can generate a growth of ability. Though each example provides evidence in one mode of language, other modes have led to that performance, as we hope to illustrate.

(a) Talk in *Kes*

Barry Hines's *Kes* provides a fictional but familiar and authentic example. Billy's care for his hawk leads him to read a technical book of a difficulty far beyond the reading ability that he has previously displayed. Billy's teacher encourages him to give a talk to his class which is far more competent than his previous performances would have led anyone to expect. The teacher allows Billy to do this by abandoning his lesson plan, and provides Billy with a real audience, one which does not know or even suspect what is to be told. The teacher shows genuine interest and he tactfully develops Billy's skill as a speaker by drawing his attention to the need to consider his audience. He does this undidactically by means of unobtrusive and genuine questions. The spontaneous applause from the class is the appropriate response to Billy's language achievement.

(b)   Reading Gorky

Our second example is of reading. Four fourteen-year-olds asked to borrow Gorky's *My Childhood* because they had enjoyed a reading from it in class. The teacher thought that they would not be able to read it themselves, but that humiliation at discovering this in private would be a lesser evil than being refused the book in public. Within a fortnight, they claimed to have read and enjoyed all 234 closely printed pages of the book, Russian names and all, at home and in lesson time. They said they found Gorky's childhood experiences far from alien, and their talk suggested they had indeed read it all and understood the gist. Here is an extract from a transcript of a shy girl, Vivienne, telling a teacher about the end of the book, a week after having been loaned the book.

She got caught on the gravestone and the cross/I think/and she split her face open/and the grandfather took her in the hut/and tried to make her better/and she was blaming everything onto herself/and all this/and she cried/and the grandfather came out to Alexei and said 'Your mother's died'/and he ran in and laid on the bed/and then the uncle/her/his stepfather came in and he got a chair and banged it on the floor and he bent over her and cried/and Alexei liked him in the end!

Here is part of the text which she is recalling:

For what seemed an eternity I stood there with the cup in

30

my hand and watched her face turn stiff, cold and grey.

When Grandfather came in I said:

'Mother's dead.'

He looked at the bed. 'Lying again, are you?'

He went over to the stove and made a deafening noise with the griddle and oven door as he drew out a pie. I looked at him, knowing full well Mother had died and wondering when it would sink in.

My stepfather arrived in a linen jacket and white cap. Without any noise he took a chair and carried it to Mother's bed, suddenly let it fall heavily on the floor and made a loud bellowing sound, like a trumpet:

'Yes, she's dead . . . look.'

Grandfather, with staring eyes, quietly shuffled away from the stove like a blind man, still carrying the griddle.

When the sand had been heaped over Mother's coffin Grandmother staggered about blindly among the graves and cut her face open on a cross. Yaz's father took her to his hut and while she was washing the wound offered her quiet words of consolation:

In Vivienne's retelling there is some confusion, some of it caused by her questioner's ignorance of the details of the story. There is an invented detail ('laid on the bed') which is plausible in a retelling — a sign of a sort of reading competence rather than of incompetence. There is detailed recall ('got a chair and banged it on the floor') and a substantial understanding of the passage which suggests that she had been moved to accomplish some demanding reading for meaning. When three teachers produced a FOG readability index (see Gilliland 1972) for the passage on which this speech is based, their scores varied from 13½ to 14¾ years. The girl, however, had been withdrawn as a remedial reader throughout her time at secondary school, and a month before her reading of the book had taken a Schonell Graded Word Test and a Neale Analysis which had assessed her reading age as 10 years 3 months and 10 years 0 months respectively. Undue respect for either of these sets of figures (or for a cloze analysis of her reading of the text which might have suggested it was at 'instructional level' for her) might have stopped a teacher lending her the book (as his subjective impression nearly did). To have done this would have deprived the girl of an unexpected performance which may well have been a breakthrough in attainment, confidence, and enjoyment in reading. The coming together of a learner's motivation, the aptness of meaning of a text, and the teacher's faith and judgment (here replaced by luck) can correct under-achievements and raise standards. Relying solely on objective tests of reading to determine the books which pupils read in school may only maintain or depress standards.

(c) Polished writing

A fifteen-year-old boy in a 'lower block' spent a week's English lessons writing and rewriting a piece, sometimes advised by his best friend, also considered weak at English. He began the piece on his own initiative and received from his teacher permission to do so, encouragement and appreciation of successive drafts, and whatever advice and correction he specifically sought (almost entirely to do with spelling). The final version was written in laborious handwriting on a spirit duplicating master then duplicated so that it could be distributed to his classmates (who had been doing other work).

Drunken Pig!

A Lonely man hovers home, From the Place where he drank away his sorrows, Sorrows of how he was going to tell his wife about the Job he had Lost. An engineer by trade. He arrived home, His wife looked at him Examining the soil dirt and greasy oil bedded tightly down in his finger nails. Plus the sorrowful look on his face. Big Sagging bags under his eyes. Blackheads deep down into his skin ready to burst. His wife washing the remainder of the pots from the previous meal. She stood in amazement still scanning her eyes over his Carcass.

He sank down breathless onto his big broad buttocks and buried his Face into his big greasy hands. His Wife spoke with a kind of Sarcastic purr. TEA OR COFFEE. He paused before reciting his order. TEA LOVE. She sat down next to him. The hot steam rose From his cup. He drank some of his

Tea even though it was a considerable strain with roughly ten pints of various makes of liquer in his insides. The affects of drinking had hit him very badly. He drank the rest of his tea pausing to belch which amused him considerably as he sat starring into the large pub mirror with the name of his Favourite alcaholic stimulate.

He was muttering to a porcelain Figure which he took with Great interest as though they were exchanging very amusing convesations with each other.

His wife watching him indulging in an activitie which he liked. So she rose from her seat and proceeded to the bedroom where she changed into her nightclothes climbed into bed and Fell into a deep sleep.

Her husband making no effort to move ended his conversation with the porcelain Figure and rolled two three times sidways and Fell, Full length on the leather couch and also fell into a deep sleep grunting like a big steam engine.

The writer was very committed to this piece. Perhaps it had a special meaning for him. The teacher refrained from meddling with 'skills' and correction. Flexible classroom arrangements allowed the writer to concentrate on it for a long time and to improve it as he worked on different drafts. The result is precise vocabulary, realized detail, wit, and technical accuracy unprecedented in his output.

SECTION 5:
IMPLICATIONS FOR ASSESSING

'Precise vocabulary, realized detail, wit, and technical accuracy' were cited as good qualities in the last piece of work. Whereas we might all perhaps be able to recognize the first three of these, and even agree that they were present or not in a piece of work, we could neither prove them nor measure them. Thus it is harder to lay down criteria for competence in a complex view of language than in a narrow view. We could not always be sure that those 'good qualities' were always good in themselves. For instance, for other purposes, in a warning, for example 'realized detail' or 'wit' might be bad qualities because in that context they would interfere with the brevity and clarity we would demand. If we asked a pupil to write instructions for others in the class on how to operate the new tape-recorder, we should value legibility, spacious lay-out, unambiguity, orderliness, conciseness, and total conformity to conventional spelling and grammar. But for another written task we might prefer humour, speed of execution, length, or use of imagery. So we cannot, in a complex view of assessment, lay down criteria which will apply generally and in every circumstance.

For any particular piece of work, however, it may be possible and helpful to suggest some criteria beforehand. We may suggest them to ourselves or we may suggest them, or imply them by means of advice to the pupils — getting pupils to internalize our criteria and standards is one objective of our teaching. However, for some work we may not correctly predict the functions or modes of the language in which the pupils realize our suggestions, and therefore we may not correctly predict the criteria for assessing it. For instance, a teacher's instructions to prepare a project on pets may be given with the expectation of receiving neat illustrated written work, but it could produce reading and spontaneous talk like Billy's in *Kes*. So, although a purposeful teacher may approach each act of assessment with a particular list of criteria he considers appropriate for that occasion, he will be open-minded and ready to recognize unanticipated but worthy performances and qualities.

Another problem in laying down criteria for language performances, such as those described in the last section, is that it requires knowledge of the pupils. Obvious instances of this are the way the teachers who respected their pupils knew that difficult work in another mode (reading), at which they were supposedly weak, was part of the process by which Billy Casper and Vivienne came to speak as they did. The teachers valued the performances because they knew they were outstanding for those pupils — they were measuring them against previous performances, not against some standardized norms. Our assessment of 'Lost in the Fog' will differ, even if we do not know the writer personally, according to whether we think it is by a demoralized adolescent or a precocious primary pupil, by a cynical sixth-former or an uneducated pensioner, by a user of English as a first language or by a user of English as a second language, by someone telling the truth or by someone making it up. Many of the questions asked in assessing 'The Day I Tort the Teachers' on the first page assumed that knowledge of the writer was important. So another implication is that assessment is often best done by a teacher with personal knowledge of the pupil. Using personal knowledge of the pupil reminds us that assessment is, either consciously or unconsciously, a continuing everyday part of teaching. Regular attention to a pupil's speech, or to his ability to read aloud, or to his writing, will provide more evidence of the language processes and development of his language uses than 'one-off' assessments, provided that some of the criteria we have been outlining are borne in mind by the teacher. Such continuous assessment is more diagnostic, because it provides an insight into the nature of the pupil's progress and problems. It is fairer, and therefore more significant, because assessment is based on a wide variety of work in authentic situations. For these reasons teacher-involvement and course work assessment, which have been a feature of some school-leaving examinations, at their best are far more valuable in assessing a pupil's abilities than traditional examination procedures.

If the criteria for assessment are to be flexible and based on the teacher's knowledge of the pupil, on evidence accumulated over a period, on an understanding of process, as well as on an analysis of product, then the assessment is more likely to be based on impression. (We have more to say about the validity and reliability of such assessment in the next chapter.) Such assessing however, needs confidence and clarity by the teacher, as well as care for, and understanding of, the pupil. Many of us may be chary of trusting our personal judgments in such important matters. But we cannot renounce our privileged positions as the experts on the language of our pupils, by refusing the responsibility and turn instead to standardized tests with all their dangers, as we have discussed in Chapter One. We can, however, do two things to justify using impression marking, and make us more confident in doing so.

First, we can clear our minds, and reinforce our confidence by openly discussing, justifying, modifying and confirming our criteria and assessments with other teachers, and, in some cases, with the pupil, with his parents, and with administrators or employers. In this way we can be sure that our judgments, though personal, can be made explicable, rationally defended, and seen to be accountable. Second, by using multiple marking in some instances, we can gain confidence and reach agreement at least about the surface features of the language products with the result that we can be more certain we have not missed or misinterpreted any aspects of the language process. Such collaborative marking disciplines our thinking about criteria, checks the rationality and accountability of our personal judgments, and provides us with a valuable exercise in in-service training, especially if we are inexperienced.

'In-service training through collaborative marking' helps to remind us of the individual differences between children, differences which can easily be forgotten, ignored, or reduced by an emphasis on insensitive and indiscriminate methods of assessing. To experience another teacher's estimate of our pupils' work can remind us that other people may interpret our evidence differently, and make us check that our interpretation is a fully-informed and impartial one. To join other teachers, perhaps more experienced than ourselves, in assessing the course work of many pupils, helps us to get a sense of what represents progress and excellence in language use, while reminding us that different pupils progress in different ways. Some knowledge of theories of learning and of child development will help us formulate reasonable expectations of children. Some abilities can only follow others, as was implied by our elements of reading in Section 1 of this chapter. If we have a list to check progress in talk, for instance, it might embody such expected directions of development as these: short utterances will precede long ones; learning to modify previous statements in the light of the listener's response is an advance on just repeating assertions; being able to talk about the past or future is an advance on being able to talk only about the present; being able to talk about the hypothetical is an advance on being able to talk only about the actual or the expected; abstract talk is built on concrete talk; being able to shape an anecdote so that its early parts gain by building on an anticipation of later ones, and later parts are enhanced by implicit or explicit references to earlier parts is a more sophisticated achievement than just being able to narrate past events in their correct sequence. But here again we must beware of being too rigid in using these signs of progress as criteria. 'Sub-vocalization' may look like progress in reading if it follows reading aloud, but it may be an obstacle in the path to fluent silent reading, since it is not always possible to read phonically — even sub-vocally — fast enough for normal reading. We know which way a child's language should advance, but it is dangerous to generalize about the speed, breadth, rhythm, or method of that advance. The development of language is more like climbing a tree than climbing a ladder. If we are too dogmatic we may push at the wrong places, or miss unexpected advances which need immediate support.

If we dictate the advance by drawing up a timetable for meeting certain developmental signposts, we make for inefficiency and underachievement. If we were to use the list of reading elements on pp. 17—18 as an expected sequence for instance, we might well miss progress in elements 3 or 6 when we were still looking out for elements 1 and 2 or 5. We might ignore children's individual differences and the part played by their individual interests and motivations in learning. Collaborative marking will broaden our conception of how much children are capable of. Stereotyped grading, or categorizing, on the other hand, may make us blind to their particular abilities and needs, and to the opportunities to help them which they present us with. A norm-referenced categorization of Billy Casper and Vivienne as poor readers would, but for chance, have deprived them of the opportunities to 'over-perform'. Constantly telling a pupil that he is poor will almost certainly limit his own self-image and efforts, and thereby put a brake on his development. One of the most limiting attitudes to, and effects of, assessment is shown when a pupil is assessed in terms of comparison to norms of theoretical excellence rather than in terms of the ways in which his reading, writing, talking and listening are succeeding, developing and still needing help.

Chapter Three:
Tests and Examinations –
and their Alternatives

In this chapter we want to make explicit our reservations about the value of tests and formal examinations, reservations which have been hinted at in the earlier chapters. Most of our examples of tests will be taken from the testing of reading, since so much more has been produced in this mode than in writing, listening or talking.

SECTION 1:
READING AND COMPREHENSION

(a)   Standardized tests

The results of standardised tests can be used to make decisions which alter people's lives. This being so, it is important to examine the claims of those who devise, publish and use them. Each test of this kind purports to measure some aspect of a pupil's language ability. The problems raised by such claims should immediately be obvious — the tests set out to investigate some internal mental process (an intellectual construct of the test designer) by examining external concrete evidence. To construct the test, the designer has to decide what it is that he is testing. He must postulate that such an 'ability' exists and can be isolated and measured. To make sure that this 'ability' and only this ability is what he is measuring, he must exclude the influence of other abilities from his measurements. In the current state of knowledge about testing language, and mental processes, what can be measured is at best limited to a few aspects of language which can be isolated. As we argued in the last chapter, some aspects are relatively trivial, whereas some more fundamental aspects of language cannot be tested or isolated.

When the limitations of tests are not recognized, claims can be made for them which are unrealistic. Cassell's *Linked English Tests*, for example, claim to provide:

> . . . Attainment Tests which measure each child's ability in
> five key areas: spelling, linguistics, vocabulary, punctuation,
> and comprehension (and identify his exact weakness).

Human knowledge is not so advanced that a test could achieve
such aims as these, and it is dangerous to claim that they can be
achieved, when teachers are understandably anxious about their
success in developing exactly those abilities which the test
claims to isolate.

The abilities which tests do measure, whether skilfully isolated or not, and whether by design or not, are largely reading
abilities. Even tests which claim to measure 'verbal ability', 'writing ability', or 'English' depend, for their administration, on
the reading abilities of the pupils being tested. Most depend, for
their reliability on the pupils' understanding of instructions
given in a precise and identically prescribed manner, and since
such instructions are usually given in a form which pupils have
to read, the tests implicitly depend upon reading competence.
At the very least they are instrumental tests of the ability to
read and understand instructions. The full language potential of
our pupils, including their talk in all its complexity and their
imaginative writing, is simply untapped by standardized testing.
Even many reading abilities, such as those associated with our
elements 5 and 6 of Chapter Two, deal with the mysteries of
what happens when we actually think and feel through language. Those are mysteries about which tests provide no information. As the Bullock Report says ' . . . reading ability has out-
stripped the available tests'. (2.34 p.33)

There are hundreds of those standardized tests which do limit
their claims to testing exclusively reading abilities (see Pumfrey
1976). We mentioned some in Chapter Two Section 1, and we
looked at the questions raised by the use of one of them in
Chapter One Section 2. Their characteristics are determined by
the view of language and of reading on which they are based.
So, then, are their *effects* on teaching.

> . . . If we think of reading primarily as a visual task, we will
> be concerned with the correction of visual defects and the
> provision of legible reading material. If we think of reading as

word recognition, we will drill on the basic sight vocabulary and word recognition skills. If we think of reading as merely reproducing we will direct the student's attention to the literal meaning of the passage and check his comprehension of it. If we think of reading as a thinking process, we shall be concerned with the reader's skill in making interpretations and generalizations, in drawing inferences and conclusions. If we think of reading as contributing to personal development and effecting desirable personality changes, we will provide our students with reading materials that meet their needs or have some application to their lives.

from Strang, McCullough and Traxler (1961) pages 8, 9

Most reading tests are devised by psychologists or teachers with expert knowledge of children with reading difficulties. So, not only are their tests and the teaching they encourage willy nilly limited to the first three or four elements of our list on pages 17–18 but they may be predisposed to treat the reading of all children as characterized by those elements which characterize the reading of children with reading difficulties. Now it could be that the importance, in the performance of *poor* readers, of certain aspects of reading is precisely what *makes* them poor readers. Perhaps in one aspect of the process they have stuck at a threshold which competent readers have passed. The ability of competent readers to overcome that particular aspect may make a relatively unimportant contribution to their overall performance and progress, once past the threshold, whereas for the weak reader it constitutes a hurdle whose importance dominates all other aspects. The analogy might be again the control of fingers in playing the piano: at a learning stage this is of critical importance, but if the player continues to concentrate on his fingers — keeps them in his focal awareness instead of allowing them to pass into subsidiary awareness — finger movement will become a hindrance to his playing.

To give examples from reading: whereas a slow reader probably decodes each word separately, a fluent reader has no time to do so. Although the fluent reader can recognize individual words, the degree of that ability is not an important determinant of his ability to read fluently. Whereas late readers may be best taught by phonics, early readers have often learnt, maybe before they go to school, to read visually: although an early reader can recode phonically, the degree of that ability is not an important determinant of his reading ability.

These examples serve to illustrate the dangers of assuming that the sort of isolated ability which any one test will measure is equally important for every pupil.

According to The Bullock Report (Table 39, p. 381), the most commonly used standardised reading tests are word-recognition tests, notably the Schonell Graded Word Reading Test which we mentioned in Chapter One. It is not strictly accurate to call such tests 'word recognition' tests, because to ensure that their words had been recognized, the tester would have to exceed the test's instructions by discussing the meanings of the words with the children being tested. To do this, however, would invalidate the test. In fact they are really 'recoding' tests, because the evidence they use is confined to the children's ability to sound-out isolated words. Thus a Portuguese boy, aged twelve, who spoke and read no English scored a Reading Age of 8.4 on the Schonell Word-Recognition Test.

There is no evidence that this recoding ability is the most important factor in reading achievement for all children. Recoding plays no part in fluent silent reading. Indeed, recoding hampers fluent silent reading since it is impossible — even at the level of 'sub-vocalization' — to sound out words as fast as they are read by competent readers. However, it is comforting to *assume* that such an ability is central to reading because that ability is testable. The use of most reading tests is based on such simplistic notions. If we use the results of the Schonell Graded Word Reading Tests or Burt's (rearranged) Word Reading Test to screen, stream, or monitor our pupils' reading progress, we assume that the ability to recognize individual words out of context is central to reading achievement. Similarly, if we use such tests as the Domain Phonic Tests or the Swansea Test of Phonic Skills without great care for their limitations and very particular applications, we may be working on an assumption that phonic knowledge is always necessary when children begin to learn to read — an assumption disproved by the way some children teach themselves to read from advertisements or labels on boxes. If we use such tests as the Widespan or the Southgate Group Reading Test, we assume that comprehension is adequately tested by requiring readers to select the one and only one word out of several to fill a gap appropriately. The assumption, in those who use such tests, that only one word is appropriate, often leads to more imaginative guesses being devalued, and may teach pupils an inflexible and limited view of language possibilities.

Standardized tests are based upon an assumption that some limited aspect of reading is of central importance to ability in English. However objective their *measurements*, the use of their results must be based upon *subjective judgments* about what is central to English. Such assumptions, together with the equally arbitrary assumption that the abilities measured by tests are normally distributed, and the inevitable tendency of test material to fall behind the progress of usage, make them dangerous guides to children's language abilities.

(b)   Comprehension tests

Another kind of test of language ability is the comprehension test. Some standardized reading tests, often tests of silent reading, are called 'comprehension tests', because the pupil must provide one-word answers or fill gaps with words, it being assumed that he can only do this if he has understood the passage. In practice, however, it may be hard to define what the pupil has understood, just as it is hard to be sure that when a word on a Schonell Graded Word Reading Test is correctly *sounded out* it has been *recognized*.

In answers to conventional comprehension exercises it is difficult to disentangle the respective contributions of understanding, lower-order ability at reading the passage, skills at writing answers to the questions, and knowledge of the often arbitrary rules of the question-and-answer game.

If this chapter had begun with the words 'In this chapter we want to arpang and make explicit our sprungnivigations about the value of aardvarks and frothing bungs . . . ' you could answer such questions as 'What is the intention of this chapter?' and 'About what does the writer have sprungnivigations?' without understanding the meaning of either the passage or the question. Your answering would, however, demonstrate that you understood something of the syntax and simple level meaning of the English language.

But there is more to comprehension of even a short passage than knowing syntax or the literal meaning of words. To comprehend a text a reader has to judge the writer's intention towards him, and evaluate the truth of what he is reading; a reader has to judge the writer's attitude towards both him, the reader, and what he is writing; the reader may also have to take into account the specific context in which the text appears. To exemplify each of these briefly: a reading of 'Guinness is good for you' which did not understand that it was intended to persuade rather than inform would be a failure of comprehension; a reading of a jokey letter as if it were hostile or serious would be dangerous; a reading of the headline 'BOYCOTT SUCCEEDS' as if it was on the sports, rather than international affairs page, would be another kind of failure to comprehend.

All those aspects of comprehension exist in the text, rather than the reader, but, there are also aspects of comprehension which depend on the reader. If the reader who notices 'BOYCOTT SUCCEEDS' is a Yorkshireman interested in cricket or South African interested in growing oranges, we make allowances for that in assessing his misunderstanding or other response. Our *purposes* in reading also affect our comprehension, so that, for example, we make different sense of the same text when we read it on different occasions. Our familiarity with the subject matter and vocabulary of a text makes a difference. So do our previous reading experiences.

Not all these aspects will be present, or equally important, in any single act of comprehension, and we shall not suggest there is a procedure for assessing comprehension which will take them all into account. However, some of the alternatives we suggest to the traditional passage and question method do provide more satisfactory ways of assessing comprehension. In our opinion, at its worst that method may test no more than two things: a familiarity with certain conventional ways of matching the structure of sentences in the passage with the structure of questions, and then merely transforming the questions and sentences to make answers; and a knowledge of the literal meanings of words. At best it tests an ability to infer the writer's attitude to his material and his reader, and possibly his intention upon the reader; though texts are not usually written with the intention of being used to test comprehension.

But three other aspects of comprehension are rarely, if ever, assessed by traditional tests. One is the use of context we have mentioned; for a piece to appear in a newspaper (illustrated, headlined, and in newsprint) affects its meaning, and immediately tells a reader something about its topicality, intentions, and seriousness; for the piece to be in an encyclopaedia, manual, or novel implies other things. Traditional comprehension passages, such as newspaper extracts, are not presented in their original printed forms, nor the reading situations for which they were originally intended.

A second aspect of comprehension not assessed by traditional tests of comprehension is an appreciation of the overall structure, shape, and development of a passage — an appreciation of what happens to the meaning of one part because it follows, and therefore takes account of, what has gone before. The tendency to set extracts, rather than whole texts, contributes to this defect, because it excludes from the process of comprehension components such as anticipating what is to follow and remembering what has passed, aspects which direct our attention to what we are reading in a special way when we read from books.

A third aspect unassessed by comprehension tests is the reader's purpose in reading the passage. To put it simply, information is for assimilating, or acting upon, instructions are for obeying, advertisements are for evaluating then yielding to or rejecting, poems and stories are for enjoying and being moved by. Comprehension passages, however, are for answering questions on; they are a form of reading behaviour divorced from the purposes of 'real-life' reading, and therefore not important to assess and not valid for basing an assessment of comprehension on. Comprehension *questions* are similarly artificial. They presuppose a purpose for reading which is artificial, and even when, in real-life, we do read to answer some sorts of questions, we have the questions formulated beforehand, whereas in traditional comprehension exercises they come after the passage.

One form of 'question' especially exemplifies the artificiality both of the role such exercises cast the reader in, and of the limited view of comprehension. That is the précis type of question. In 'real reading', our comprehension of a text, even when it does result in some restatement (and it may more appropriately result in enjoyment, action, or dismissal) is more likely to be an expansion, a verbatim reproduction, an assimilation into a statement of some personal concern, or a few scribbled notes, than a statement in continuous prose of the main points of the original in the original order at one third of the length. To insist on summarizing of this kind is almost always to teach an inappropriate and indiscriminate reading style, and is an example of testing which is not helpful. Some of the suggested alternatives to testing which follow are more likely to encourage those forms of comprehension which in real life pupils will need to develop.

(c)   Assessing reading and comprehension without using tests
We now describe just three ways of assessing reading and comprehension which we think are more valuable than tests. In each case, the procedure we describe provides the teacher with information (but not quantified measurement) which he can use to diagnose problems, screen out individuals for special attention, or monitor the progress of individuals. In each case the procedure involves the pupils in activities from which they, as well as the teacher, will learn.

(i)   Gaining an overview of the reading progress of a whole class
A simple way of scanning the reading of all members of a class at once is to give them all copies of a reader of appropriate interest and which most of them are able to read. The teacher tells them to begin reading silently at the first page. For fifteen minutes, he watches out for, and may note:
   which pupils move their lips, follow with their fingers or use rulers under the lines;
   which pupils have concentrated on reading for the whole of the fifteen minutes;
   which pupils seem disaffected by reading;
   which pupils struggle but persevere, and which struggle and

give up.

After fifteen minutes the teacher stops the class and records the number of pages read by each pupil. That record gives a rough indication of the pupils' speeds of reading and/or their interests in the text.

Then the teacher gives out individual copies of a cloze procedure text derived from the first two pages of the book and asks the pupils to complete them individually. A reading of their completions will show the teacher:

> which pupils have read sensitively enough, and remember the original vividly enough, to complete the passage with the original words or with words with the same style and feel;
>
> which pupils can complete the passage competently;
>
> which pupils cannot supply appropriate words.

The teacher now has two pieces of information about most children — one about their reading speed and style, and one about their comprehension.

Now he can go on to ask them to finish reading the book in the next fortnight. In that time he notes which pupils finish the book. He may find, for instance, that some low-scorers on the cloze exercise may finish quickly, showing they have an ability like that which Vivienne displayed to commit themselves to a particular book in a way that may overcome basic handicaps. The teacher also talks to the pupils about their reading of the book and makes assessments of their reading attitudes (and the suitability of the book for them), from their eagerness and comments on individual parts.

An overview of this kind can also be made of non-narrative reading. The teacher may make additional observations here, such as which pupils turn back to reread, and which use index, dictionaries, and other reference apparatus. With older pupils he may note their use, and methods, of note-making.

(ii) Screening of those pupils in need of special help with reading

The case-history we shall use for our second example had wider purposes than the screening we shall concentrate on, since the operation was conducted by a secondary Head of English new to her school who was anxious to gain an overview of the reading ability of her pupils and to alert her department to their reading behaviour and needs, as well as to screen out those with particular difficulties. She used a procedure more time-consuming than that of our first example, but one which allows sensitive individual diagnosis of problems and fosters good relationships with pupils.

A series of passages of graded difficulty were prepared using a 'readability formula', and teachers were asked to hear their own pupils read these individually. As they listened, the teachers noted the readers' 'miscues' (hesitations, repetitions, omissions, mispronunciations and so on) by putting agreed symbols on parallel duplicated texts. Examples of the use of this sort of reading record will be found in Melnik and Merritt (1972a), Pumfrey (1976) and Longley (1977) under the headings 'Miscue analysis' or 'Informal reading inventories'. Teachers who are beginners find it helpful to tape-record the readings, and annotate the texts, whilst playing back the recordings. The point at which reading the passages becomes painfully difficult gives the teacher some indication of a pupil's degree of difficulty (and a warning when to stop), and helps with the screening. The analysis of the recorded 'miscues' for a pupil with reading difficulties may tell the teacher a good deal (increasingly so with experience) about the nature, causes and possible cures for such difficulties. The technique allows the spotting of many problems which tests would not reveal. On one of the 'Reading after Ten' broadcasts, for example, (see Longley 1977) one can hear a teacher realizing that a child is mistaking meaning because he does not appreciate the intention and effect of speech marks. Furthermore, the teacher can add background to a miscue analysis by discussing each reading with the reader, and asking questions about the particular text and about the pupil's reading in general. The use of checklists such as are described later in this chapter can help to inform such discussion.

In her departmental memo on compiling these 'informal reading inventories' and screening out pupils with special difficult-ies, the Head of Department from whom we have this case-history stresses the need to find each pupil's individual reading difficulties, rather than a general reading age for each one, so that individual help can be given. She also stresses that one criterion by which the passages were chosen was that they might lead to discussion and a desire to read the books from which they came.

(iii) Assessing and teaching comprehension by using 'prepared' texts

Comprehension needs imaginative abilities, such as to anticipate events, and to infer intentions, as well as the analytical abilities tested by traditional comprehension exercises. Here are three simple procedures which teach such use of the imagination in reading and help the teacher assess it.

First, there is the use of cloze procedure referred to above. Pupils' efforts to guess deleted words direct their attention to using clues, especially retroactive ones, to infer unfamiliar or skipped words in 'clean' texts, as well as providing evidence for the teacher assessing the ability to use such clues. It is the ability to infer in this manner that pupils need to learn in order to cope with both difficult texts with unfamiliar words in them, and with fast reading which skips words. It is also an interesting alternative to 'comprehension questions' for drawing the attention of pupils to the way poetry works, especially where rhyme, rhythm, and tone have to be taken into account to provide appropriate fillers for gaps.

Second, there is the presentation of the paragraphs of a text in random order. The ability to sort out a meaningful order for the paragraphs provides education in, and evidence for the assessing of, the ability to comprehend such features of sequential structure as the way an author builds on what has gone before, so that later paragraphs take account of earlier ones, or of the function of adverbs or collocations of words (like 'furthermore', or 'a further example of what we have said') which refer the reader forwards or backwards, or to a turning point in a text. Such 'sequencing' also takes account of the overall shaping of a literary text, a shaping which is ignored both by the assumptions behind the marking of 'Lost in the Fog' and by traditional comprehension tests and exercises, so that it is particularly relevant to the study of poems and stories, though not as a replacement for consideration of the affective aspects of literary works, of course. Paradoxically it is also applicable to the teaching and assessing of reading of technical instructions. Where sequence is all-important (as in technical instructions), for the reader to have to make that sequence is often the best way for him to have his attention drawn to its importance and to the essential part played by each step.

A third use of 'prepared texts', especially applicable to the comprehension of stories, is prediction. Here, the pupil is given a complete text only in separated instalments. After a reading of each instalment he has to predict what will come next before he can collect the next instalment to read and check his prediction. The process of anticipating, self-checking, readjusting the overall picture, and predicting with increasing speed and confidence — a 'whole-text' parallel to the comprehension of difficult sentences — is an essential step on the way to assured reading, and it provides evidence from which the teacher can see what help is needed. This provides a large-scale parallel to miscue analysis, in that it is one way of seeing into the reading process as it takes place, rather than inferring it from *post facto* evidence.

Such prediction is a valuable *group* activity, too, because the sharing of the activity makes the reading seem enjoyable and 'normal', and because the discussions necessarily involved in group prediction help each pupil to recognize the clues available. Group activity is also valuable in the use of cloze procedure and in 'sequencing' as well. To conduct them as group activities may make administrative difficulties for the assessor, but it makes the activities more helpful experiences for the learner.

SECTION 2:
WRITTEN EXAMINATIONS

(a) Impression marking

Assessments of writing — often in numerical terms — are the staple of examining and grading in secondary schools. Because this is so, it is easily forgotten that most of the assessment of children's writing in schools is a matter of personal judgment. It is true that correctness of spelling can be measured, and so to some extent can correctness of punctuation and conformity to the grammar of Standard English. More sophisticated attempts to quantify the complexities of writing are described in Chapter Five of Moffett (1968) and in the first half of Wilkinson (1978). But it is rarely helpful to children for their writing to be assessed merely on its spelling, punctuation, grammar, or sentence structure. If we do assess like this, we should make it clear that we are using the writing to assess spelling or whatever, and we are not assessing the quality of the writing itself. Otherwise pupils can be discouraged from using writing for grappling with difficult ideas or for other worthwhile purposes. When we assess writing we take its quantifiable surface features into account, but we also take into account its non-quantifiable surface features, such as handwriting, and more profound features, such as its meaning, care, and imagination, which we discussed in Chapter Two. Usually, even quantifiable features (such as grammar or syntactical complexity) are assessed on 'impression' rather than by counting. The ubiquity of impression marking is sometimes disguised by 'analytical marking' or the use of marking schemes. For instance, one of the two markers of each essay for the JMB GCE O level English Language Syllabus A examination has an analytical marking scheme (the other has an equal number of marks to allocate globally on impression). The analytical marker allocates his marks as follows: a fifth for mechanical accuracy; a fifth for content; a fifth for planning, development, paragraphing, and so on; a fifth for expression; and a fifth for general impression excluding mechanical accuracy. (Those are a summary of the Board's full instructions.) For mechanical accuracy a method of 'mistake-counting' is specified. The fifth category is overtly impressionistic. But then three other categories, qualities of content, development, and expression, are impressionistic too: they roughly correspond to what we have called 'meaning', 'shaping' (in our comments on 'Lost in the Fog') and 'appropriateness of register' and 'tone'. The analytical marking scheme determines the relative *weightings* of the qualities (and those weightings are themselves value judgments), but it cannot stop the marking of those qualities (and therefore of four-fifths of the marking) being as impressionistic as the marking of the 'impression marker', or of the teacher operating the Board's Syllabus D who, to assess his pupils' course work, is provided with criteria which are detailed but still a matter of personal judgment and not susceptible to measurement.

Such inevitable impression marking can be a cause of insecurity and can lead to a reliance on misleading numerical indices such as Moffett describes, or to an over-emphasis on the apparently quantifiable surface features. We should prefer that the personal nature of the assessment of writing was recognized, protected and made accountable by a discussion, clarification, and declaration of the criteria used, as happens in the JMB's syllabus D. Experienced markers can grade work with confidence so that there will be mutual agreement on the grade. That this is so is suggested by what happens in the 'agreement trials' which CSE and GCE Boards hold, or the check by secondary English departments of the consistency of their grades, or in the discussions of primary teachers to compare pupils' writings.

Britton, Martin and Rosen (1966) compared the marks given on impression by teams of teachers to O level compositions for the Cambridge Board with those given to the same compositions by the Board's markers, who were working singly and using a marking scheme. They found the impression markers' marks were more reliable and valid than those of the 'official' markers — that is they correlated better with other marks obtained the same way and with assessments of the pupils' abilities at composition based on school work. This experiment may have been influential in making multiple-impression marking acceptable in CSE Mode 3 examinations, then in their infancy, and it is timely to be remined of the pragmatic utility of impression marking when there is the likelihood of innovatory 16+ examination schemes.

It is noteworthy that it was *multiple*-impression marking which was matched with individual analytical marking, and the use of a team (or a pair) of markers is a sensible precaution in impression marking against assessment being grossly distorted by carelessness, poor judgment, or bias in a marker. It is also a wise tactic to publicize the fact that such a precaution is being taken, so that older students do not fear, as some may, that their results may be jeopardized by the bias of a teacher on whose assessment they are wholly dependent. It is also a luxury which the speed of impression-marking allows, compared with more traditional kinds of marking. Furthermore, as implied in Section 3, it is a way of training inexperienced teachers.

(b) Personal judgment

It is a fact that impression marking of writing does work (and this also applies to the assessment of talk and response to reading). A great deal of our apparently objective knowledge is really subjective (witnesses in court prove that) and most of what we use to make meaning comes from inside us. But subjective judgment is still susceptible to reason and discussion, even if there can never be total certainty and agreement. Our judgments are expressed in language and language is common, in the sense that our use of it aspires to common meanings and common standards. Just as, although we may have different tastes in food, we may discuss them and agree on what is nutritious, well-cooked, or poisonous, so may we modify and discipline our personal judgments by our common aspirations. That way, we keep them rational, responsible, and defensible. Thus qualities of writing such as 'sincerity' and 'vigour' may be invoked as criteria of assessment, even though they are not quantifiable. If we remain sensitive and attentive to such qualities and to each other, we can recognize and agree on them rather than abandon concern for them because they appear vague.

When we are concerned with the full range of powers of language, we must protect our sensitivities to its nuances. If we are to assess children's language responsibly, we must practise what we preach by talking, writing, and reading to our own limits, with sincerity, vigour, meaning, care, and imagination. If, for instance, teachers of literature are discriminating readers and try their hands at 'creative' and 'personal' writing themselves, they will find it easier to distinguish enlivening from mechanical detail in children's writing, even though there is no *measure*, nor certain instrumental test, for doing so. Just as with reading, if our assessment of children's writing relies on the certainty of figures or only takes account of the surface features, we will ultimately devalue children's writing. It is as if we were to judge Shakespeare's plays by the variations in his spelling. Crude and partial assessments of writing will ultimately encourage a crude and partial practice of writing and a fall in standards. The

52

nature and importance of taking into account those qualities which can only be assessed by personal judgment is suggested by the definition of intuition in Smith (1973):

a responsiveness to the intangible forces and motivations that largely determine the manifest nature of events . . . (p. 196)

(c) Assessing the writing of a class without a formal examination

How might impression marking, secured by such collaborative procedures as multiple marking and discussion of meanings and standards, be used to produce what examinations demand without the drawbacks of examinations? (By 'drawbacks' we mean their limiting the writing assessed to timed pieces from a limited range of topics under anxiety-inducing conditions for an unknown audience.) It depends on the age of the pupils and the constraints on the teacher. Let us take as an example a secondary English department required to produce examination results for third-year pupils, so that sets can be made up for next year's courses, but the department is free to derive those results by any method it chooses. Suppose members of that department are used to working together — to different extents according to their inclinations and experiences. Perhaps some have been involved in the school's CSE Mode 3 assessments of writing and talk and some have team-taught or collaborated in editing magazines of children's writing. The first decision they might make is what weighting the work in different modes of language might have in their 'exam substitute'. They would want the overall result in English to reflect ability in reading and talk as well as writing, and they might want to enlist the school librarian or drama specialist in their assessments. But they would want the result to reflect work in a way which allowed the components to be separated and even sub-divided — so that, for instance, a pupil's private reading could be given special attention in deciding whether or not to allot him to a set to study literature for an external examination. However, suppose they have decided to give writing a mark of two-fifths in the overall assessment. Then the teachers must decide what sort of writing will contribute to these marks, and how it is to earn these marks.

They may come up with a set of *purposes* for writing, a set of

53

forms of writing with those purposes, and a set of *criteria* for judging examples of those forms of writing. For third-year children in a secondary school they may look for writing with these purposes:

1 it records information for the writer's own use
2 it records information for someone else's use
3 it helps the writer to sort out his own experiences and thoughts
4 it helps the writer to understand the experiences of others
5 it symbolises experience in particular ways
6 it describes
7 it instructs
8 it seeks to persuade.

Without such purposes being defined, there can be no assessment of the success of writing.

The forms in which writing with such purposes might be embodied might include these:

1 rough notes (in any subject)
2 reports of experiments or summaries of non-narrative reading material
3 anecdotal or reflective personal writing, or writing to plan an activity
4 imaginative recreation of events in literature — from another character's point of view, and so on
5 poems, plays, stories
6 descriptions of scenes, objects, events, or operations
7 written instructions
8 letters, and written formulations of opinion.

Without practising such forms of writing in English, the teachers might feel they had not encouraged an adequate range and variety of work.

The *criteria* by which writing for these purposes and in these forms might be judged will vary according to the purposes (not, in this case, according to the writers — since the purpose of the *assessment* is for discrimination between children). In forms 2, 5, 6 and 7, surface features like orderly layout, neat handwriting and conventional spelling will be important, as will paragraphing, sub-heading, and in some cases sequence and conciseness. Some of those may not be as important in 1, although

54

speed will be important there. In some writing in form 3, an explicitness and a logical sequence and coherence, which elsewhere might seem pedantic, will be valued. In the stories of form 5, consistency of persona, tense, and feeling will be important. Tone and sense of audience will be critical in 8.

To arrive at even such incomplete lists as these will need a good deal of discussion. To set an examination to cover that range of writing would be an impracticable task. To set separate exercises for all the items, even if spread over the year, would also be laborious. Such continual and repeated examining could harm relationships between pupils and teachers, since the pupil could feel that the teacher had become an omnipresent examiner with whom he dare not take risks or make mistakes. In such a situation most pupils would, presumably, prefer the rarity and impersonality of a single 'one-off' examination, whatever the anxiety it caused and risks it entailed.

However, it is not difficult to *collect* the evidence of that range of writing, with the knowledge and collaboration of the pupil, from the corpus of the writing he has produced in the natural process of learning over a period of time.

Evidence of writing with purpose 1 is open to the teacher's observation and subject to such instrumental tests as 'can he write up his summary of a topic (writing with purpose 2) from the notes he has made from his reading or from the teacher's talk?' Concrete evidence of writing with purposes 4, 5 and 6 will be present in the pupil's exercise book or folder (and its scrutiny in examinations — such as is being described here — helps to preserve such types of writing from neglect). So the *material* for this sort of 'examination' is 'course work' (the body of recent 'public' writing) plus the records of 'continuing assessment' (the teacher's observation of writing behaviour and of the outcomes of 'private writing'). Such material may well include the range of writing set in traditional examinations — stories, descriptions, letters and formulations of opinion are all common in these. Some of the 'course work' may have been written, just as in 'examination conditions', as if for an audience of strangers, and to a time-limit, as a result of decision on the part of the department to value and practise such work.

In the next section we shall discuss the use of checklists to aid personal judgment. A checklist could be made of the purposes, forms of writing, and criteria, which we have just discussed. However, except for a very experienced team of teachers, it may be cumbersome to use and may lead to a too rigid approach that allows no credit for the unexpected in the way we described in discussing criteria in Section 5 of Chapter Two. We think these suggestions would serve their purpose by informing a department's discussion on a year's writing and on 'examining' it, with an experienced member of the department providing samples.

In practice it may be sufficient to allocate marks out of only five, for 'imaginative' and 'technical' categories of writing. This, like all examination procedures, is very crude, but if the marks were discussed against a framework of an analysis like the one above, it would be a way of involving the more sensitive judgments of teachers.

In this case, teachers in pairs, scrutinising particular pieces of work, could give their pupils marks out of five (crudely rationed), in each of these two categories, basing their marks on the previous two terms' work and on each individual teacher's records. They could call for third opinions where they disagreed. These marks could be added to those for various types of reading and oral work to make a mark out of twenty-five. A senior member of the department could 'moderate' the marks of each class (scaling them up or down or stretching their range), using a sample of written work as evidence. This leads to such instructions to the class teacher as 'Having compared a sample of your class's written work with samples of other classes, and assuming the range of ability of your class at written work is representative of the range at other work, I think you should adjust your marks — overall, not just for writing — as follows: keep your lower-than-average marks the same, upgrade your average marks by one, your better-than-average marks by two, and your best marks by 3.' Multiplication by four of the total to produce the percentages which many secondary schools require will leave 'three mark gaps' which the individual teachers can use at their discretion to correct any injustices which they feel these crude procedures may have caused, to give credit to progress (since this form of examination has a predictive purpose), or to bump up every pupil's mark so that none get discouragingly low percentages.

However, at this stage the department may feel that having climbed up this numerical ladder they can now kick it away and draw up their own collective 'order of merit' or 'groups' within the percentage framework required, working only from their newly-informed-and-confident personal judgment.

Such an 'examination', whatever its drawbacks, has four merits. First, being based on work the pupils have already done, it does not waste their time in activities from which they may not learn, and it produces results which reflect their full range of language performances undistorted by the anxieties of 'examination conditions'. Second, it offers an exercise in defining objectives and criteria for the teachers, and a guide to them in their range of work. Third, its results, though ostensibly crude grades or percentages, can be analysed into components which enable profiles of pupils' work in English to be drawn up. Such profiles are useful to pupils for directing their energies, to teachers in recommending further work or external examination entries, and to parents in interpreting reports. Finally, it opens the way to enlisting the participation of teachers of subjects other than English in the assessment of children's language, since they have evidence of success at some of the forms of writing to be assessed.

SECTION 3:
FOUR MORE AIDS TO
PERSONAL JUDGMENT

In this chapter and the last we have mentioned collaboration as an aid to the exercise of personal judgment in assessing. Without such an exercise of judgment some assessment is misleading and unhelpful. Collaborative assessment of written work protects the rationality and responsibility of such assessment. It makes criteria, description, and evaluation clear, explicit, and couched in a language whose meanings are commonly understood.

We shall conclude this chapter by describing three more aids to that inevitable exercise of personal judgment. They may be applicable to any of the three modes of language, but we have introduced them here because they illustrate the view of assessing which we introduced in the last section on writing. That view is that assessment needs a clear statement of criteria and should produce a publicly accountable description of performance.

As an introduction, consider this extract from a letter which accompanies a junior school report. It is headed 'How to Read a Report':

> Your child's report is the result of many hours of marking and recording by a team of teachers. Assessments are based on the total marks earned for work and tests done throughout the half year in each subject area. When totalled the highest (best) 10% are graded 10, the next 10% are graded 9, the next 10% are graded 8, and so on. (See codes at bottom of each report.)
>
> Some parents expect their children to 'go up a grade' in the next report. This can only be done by displacing someone else as the number of grades awarded are strictly rationed as detailed above. This should provide some incentive for competition . . .

The teachers who wrote the reports which this letter accompanied were conscientious members of a staff with great concern for the pupils' welfare. It is a sign of that concern that a letter should accompany the reports explaining the school's criteria. However, we think the wording of this letter has implications which destroy that link between assessing and helping pupils which we tried to establish at the end of Chapter One. The pupil-activity reported on seems like mutual competition rather than individual development, far less mutual cooperation. The information which the report is based on includes tests, as well as, and distinct from, learning. The assessments on the report refer to norms (levels of ability for children of that age at that school) which will mean little to most readers of the reports, rather than referring to particular criteria, such as, for writing, 'can he write his name?' 'can he copy the teacher's writing?' 'can he write sentences of his own invention?' or to the pupil's progress. The 'rationing' justified in the letter is misleading. To a layman, if not a statistician, it *is* reasonable for pupils to 'go up a grade' if they improve, since what is recorded on the report should represent their progress, rather than their place in a pecking order. The *effect* of such a report — whatever its good *intentions* — must be to depress many children who do not improve their grades or consistently earn high grades, and it must be to suggest that school exists for competition rather than learning.

The letter rightly stresses how hard the teachers have worked to produce the report. Sadly we think that much of that work will have been wasted, since its products (the grades) are misleading and unhelpful, and since the time and effort could have been put to better use. Descriptions of four aids which follow may all be time-savers for conscientious teachers, as well as instruments of more valid and accurate assessment of children's language.

(a) Assessing by observation

The report with the letter we have quoted (it looks like an elaboration of that on p. 93 of The Plowden Report) is sub-divided into 'Reading' and 'Written', with a box alongside for two marks out of ten and a space about three inches by half an inch for comments on both. Yet the teachers who wrote such reports have access to information which could provide a far more meaningful, helpful, and comprehensive report on each child's language development than this one. This brings us to the first of our four more aids to using personal judgment in assessment, with a view to establishing conscious and purposeful observation.

A teacher who is making assessment an everyday, continuing, conscious part of teaching is presented all the time with evidence of pupils' language, behaviour, attitudes, abilities and needs. An alertness to this, and a systematic way of recording and analysing it can replace the apparatus of testing. For instance, just to note the spellings for which a child asks a teacher during free writing can provide the teacher with an assessment of the child's spelling, without the use of a test. Such an assessment can be used for diagnosing what types of words, weaknesses or misunderstandings are causing the child to lack confidence in spelling. We saw how a class tackling a new class reader can help the watchful teacher with assessment. Finally, in the normal run of school administration, a primary school teacher will willy-nilly collect such important evidence of a child's progress in talk as the clarity of his speech, his ability to relate his own experiences, his ability to explain, and his ability to convey a message, or listen and respond to instructions, and so on.

Such evidence is too often ignored in favour of more standardised information which, though it may appear to dignify and quantify the assessment of children's language, really confuses it. Just to look at a page of a child's writing alongside one from a year before is a better indicator of progress than a test result or some quasi-objective measure of improvement. The provision by junior schools for secondary schools (or the requirement from junior schools by secondary schools) of grades and reading ages does less service to teachers and pupils than would the provision of a page of each child's personal writing, a page of notes by the teacher on his talk, and a counter-signed list of books he has read in the last year. This last item is a good example of something which can be used as evidence without being a measurement, and, since it indicates amount of reading and interests, it may be a more valid indicator of reading ability than the result of a standardized test. (What the Bullock Report says on language continuity – in 14.11, p. 217 – is admirable and relevant. Less admirable is this comment from page 10 of Hodder and Stoughton's pamphlet *Keeping Track of Testing* by F. A. Spooncer: 'a major skill of any teacher lies in selecting the right test materials to match his pupils' abilities'. We would say that any teacher with the skill to know his pupils' abilities would not need test materials.)

(b) Instrumental tests

Observation of learning may represent more effective assessment, and be protected against prejudice, if it is systematized. Miscue analysis is a systematization of observation. At their best, some uses of standardized tests can aid such systematization and provide checks on observation, perhaps directing a teacher to look again at some behaviour where the standardized test and the teacher's observations seem at odds. The danger is that standardised testing may replace observation. Simpler tests of learning are 'instrumental tests', observations of some simple behavioural outcomes from which a learning process or an achieved ability can be inferred. We have mentioned some of these earlier. Fluent reading tests word-recognition; being able to read the instructions of a reading test often tests reading ability as well as the test itself; a pupil completing a book provides more valuable information for most purposes than his reading age or the readability index of the book; an infant's ability to understand and make himself understood through speech shows he has an instrumental knowledge of almost all the grammar his secondary teachers may try to 'teach' him ten years later; a pupil selecting and illustrating a poem may demonstrate a better appreciation of it than by answering questions on it; using an index demonstrates a knowledge of the alphabet; using a library to draw, accurately and unaided, a picture of how the area where a pupil lives must have looked like 500 years ago demonstrates research skills. These are the commonsense tests of everyday life which a policy ·of systematic observation will value — and which will in some cases make standardized tests unnecessary.

(c) Self-assessment

Children have different learning styles and needs, and the interests and previous experiences which they bring to their learning make great differences to what they learn in using language. To understand fully what a child makes of language, what he 'comprehends' in 'comprehension', for instance, we would need to be mind readers. But although pupils may be less skilled than we are as diagnosticians and prescribers, they do have one advantage here. Even if they cannot clarify and verbalize them, they directly apprehend their needs and intentions and the extents to which they feel they are met. This information is an aid to the teacher's personal judgment, and can be partially enlisted by allowing some indirect and direct procedures to self-assessment. Such procedures are teaching instruments, since they set the pupil on the way to becoming an independent learner, and to internalizing his teacher's criteria or clarifying his own.

At its simplest, such self-assessment is enlisted when we ask pupils how they feel about their progress and problems, or allow them to choose what to do in our classes. For some self-assessing, pupils can use the very aids to personal judgment which this section recommends for teachers. Collaboration in assessment by teachers has its parallel in pupils using each other as first or final readers and judges of their work. When we enlist a pupil who is not easily embarrassed in an instrumental test of language by asking him to read an amusing piece of his writing to us or to the class, we may note from his reading whether or not he is aware that he is using sentences even though he has not shown that by the use of full stops. *He* may note how useful it would have been to him to put in those full stops, and he may thus perform an act of self-assessment through observation. A pupil's choice to finish a novel which we have introduced him to is an instrumental self-test of appreciation. Finally, looking forward to the fourth aid to personal judgment, we shall recommend that pupils, especially older ones, can use checklists to record and plan their work, either on their own or in collaboration with the teacher. The teacher will use the pupils' completed lists to guide his allocation of individual assignments or his planning of a class programme of work. If each pupil regularly fills in a questionnaire on which he records such information as the language activities he is enjoying, feels confident at, is conscious of neglecting, feels in need of help with, is finding difficult, wishes to do more of, wishes to revise or complete, how he likes being assessed and so on, he provides the teacher with valuable material for diagnosing, screening, monitoring, and planning. But he also increases his own awareness of himself as a learner — has his attention drawn to what he should do, without the intervention of the teacher and sets himself on the road to becoming the independent learner we aim to make each pupil.

(d) Using checklists to guide personal observation

Such a questionnaire would be a crude form of checklist, a systematic aide-memoire, and tool for raising awareness. Checklists can be made of questions which can be given 'yes' or 'no' answers, rather like those which pilots use before take-off, or they can be made of categories which indicate what should be observed and described.

There are good examples of ready-made checklists in some of the books we recommend. Pages 21 and 22 of Longley (1976) reproduce an admirable checklist 'Language Record' from a primary school. Joan Tough (1976) shows how a checklist can be one way of recording the functions of infants' talk (page 80). On reading, there are such checklists, like the one on reading readiness by Downing and Thackray on pages 453–4 of Melnik and Merritt (1972a), and a very practical one on pages 126 and 127 of Kohl (1974). Pages 75–9 of Longley (1977) reproduce checklists of reading motivation, oral reading faults, and higher order reading skills for use by secondary teachers when developing reading.

However, there is a good deal of value to be gained by teachers constructing their own checklists. To do so provides them with an exercise in clarifying their values, purposes, priorities, and terminology. This is especially the case when it is a collaborative exercise. Some checklists which are devised to aid assessment of secondary pupils can be devised in collaboration with the pupils. For instance, external examination entrants can learn the requirements by helping their teachers to devise lists of the criteria which will be applied to different types of writing. The teacher can then respond to pieces of writing by returning them with partially filled-in copies of the appropriate checklists.

Three uses of checklists deserve special emphasis. One is for diagnosis. Observation systematized by reference to a checklist can often lead to discovery of weaknesses without resort to standardized tests or formal examinations. That a pupil needs glasses may not be revealed by a reading test nor occur to a teacher before he is reminded, by reference to a checklist, that this may be an explanation of reading difficulty. A checklist of different types of spelling errors against which to check those mistakes in a child's writing may help to diagnose the cause of errors and therefore offer appropriate help (see Torbe 1977 p.5; 1978 p.5).

A second use of checklists is for recording progress. The 'Language Record' on pages 21–22 of Longley (1976) offers one such example. Such records are essential if talk is to be assessed. Talk is omitted from the headings of the junior school report described at the beginning of this section. This is partly because it is only relatively recently that talk has received as much attention as reading and writing, and there exist for talk neither standardized tests such as there are for reading nor formal examining procedures as there are for writing (though there is a danger of an over-emphasis on the most easily-controlled procedure of 'making a speech to a stranger' in CSE oral examining). So assessment of talk is impressionistic because there is no other method available and, as such, is valuably assisted by the use of checklists. We found one simple but useful checklist for older pupils in this list of criteria devised for teachers to use in assessing the 'Statements' in talks in CSE examinations (not necessarily in English):

(a) amount, selection and accuracy of information/ideas given
(b) quality of arrangement and intelligibility of presentation
(c) use of technical terms, extension of idea, and comparison and association
(d) relevance of the whole to:
      (i) the subject of the talk
      (ii) the objectives of the syllabus
      (from West Midlands Examination Board Memorandum No 9: *Oral Assessment in Mode 3 courses*, September 1976)

. The third special use of checklists as an aid to using personal judgment brings us back to the introduction to this section, namely their use in writing reports. Where the items on a checklist become the categories under which the pupil's language uses are described for parents, employers, or schools to which pupils transfer the report becomes a 'profile'. Such a profile has advantages over a set of grades. If its wording is simple and careful, it is far more intelligible and informative. It does not appear to categorize and limit the pupil or make him a statistical phenomenon, but describes him as the developing individual that he is. It does not appear to lay claim to any precision which is not inherent in the words it uses. It does not lump together very different language behaviours under such blanket categories as 'Reading' and 'Written', and it allows a user to pick his own selection of assessments for his particular purposes, which may be specially useful for an employer seeking a clerk or salesgirl, for instance.

Here is just a section from one profile report sent to us. The comprehensiveness of its headings allows the teachers to confine themselves largely to putting ticks on it. The teacher who submitted it described it as 'an attempt to describe rather than measure' and emphasized that the use of the profile was intended to be valuable in directing the teachers' observations, as well as in conveying information to parents. She also emphasized that it was a very provisional attempt, far from perfect. We think it worth including because it may encourage other teachers to devise their own.

CLASSWORK

(a)   **Reading**
   (i)   *General reading habits*

reads an average amount	☐
a great deal	☐
very little	☐
reading is restricted to fiction of one type	☐
to non-fiction of one type	☐
covers fiction of several types	☐
non-fiction of several types	☐
the level of difficulty attempted is average	☐
below average	☐
above average	☐
particular interests are.	

   (ii)   *Group reading scheme*

	the response to what to read is enthusiastic		☐
	interested		☐
variable	☐	neutral	☐
	apathetic		☐
	hostile		☐
	appreciation of what is read is mature		☐
	critical		☐
variable	☐	common-sense	☐
	confused		☐
	slight		☐

Chapter Four:
What to do in Practice

So far we have suggested a particular view of the purposes, the appropriate methods, and the effects of assessments of children's language, and we have hinted at guidelines we should follow in assessing children's language. In this final chapter we will restate those guidelines and consider how they might assist in the assessing problems we have used as examples. We shall then return to the four assessing situations which we outlined at the beginning and see how those guidelines apply to them.

SECTION 1:
SOME GUIDELINES

(a) Be clear about the purposes of assessment

The first guideline was implicit in the first chapter. All assessment has a function. Even at its most unconscious, assessment meets expectations, provides a ritual, or maintains a tradition. If its functions are clear and purposeful, it is possible to pick methods for assessing with discrimination, and to judge the success of the assessment by its effects. If purposes are not clear, increased effort may do harm. Amongst the purposes of assessing we have referred to have been:

diagnosing the language problems of individual pupils or of groups

monitoring their progress

screening out individuals for special help

planning appropriate work in language for individuals or groups

describing children's language for the information of parents, teachers, or other agencies

grading children's language to meet parental expectations, to predict examination performances, to guide discriminatory treatment in school or further education, or in selection for employment.

Behind those purposes lies an aspect of the value judgment that makes us teachers: assessment, like all teaching, should *help pupils to learn*.

The purpose of the teacher in assessing 'Lost in the Fog' seemed to be to cut the writer down to size, and to point out his deficiencies. A more helpful purpose would have been to recognize, acknowledge, and praise the achievement of a sensitive sustained narrative by a pupil with obvious linguistic difficulties. An assessment of 'Drunken Pig', Vivienne's reading of Gorky, or Billy Casper's talk on his kestrel could aim to record the care and meaning a pupil, given real opportunity and motivation, could achieve. Those would be opportunistic assessments. Assessments which set their purposes beforehand, and stuck to them, were exemplified by our 'writing examination alternative' (pp. 53—57) where methods of examining and recording are used which would fulfil such initial purposes as assessing the ability to use writing in examination courses and under external examination conditions.

There were also predetermined purposes for our two case-histories of assessing reading without tests, (pp. 45—48): each aimed to encourage pupils to read whilst providing the teacher with an overview of attitudes and abilities and a guide to individual differences. Perhaps the most striking indicator of the importance of clear purpose in our examples was that of the junior school report (pp. 58—59). Its form suggested that the purpose of the tests and marking on which it was based was to grade children with respect to each other, so that parents and pupils would recognize each pupil's place in an order of merit, rather than his individual progress, special successes or needs in language.

Unless teachers are clear about purposes of assessment, much of it is a waste of pupils' and teachers' time. Some assessment may have no purpose, or a purpose which is of no direct of indirect help to pupils. The first question to be asked of any particular assessment is, '*Is this procedure necessary*?' Furthermore, unless the purpose of assessment is clear, the *method* is random and may be inappropriate, and the *results* may be misleading.

(b)   Use the method of assessment appropriate to your purpose
This guideline is a direct consequence of teachers clarifying
their purposes for assessing. Different methods are appropriate
for different purposes. We have suggested that to make a record
of the novels a pupil has read recently is a more appropriate
method of assessment of his reading than to give him a standardized reading test; a profile is more appropriate for assessing
suitability for employment than a score; producing a sample of
work is more appropriate for liaison between schools than merely to exchange reading ages.

We have suggested some broad principles for choosing appropriate methods of assessment: assessing is best when it is a continuing, conscious part of teaching, for instance, or uses techniques which enlist contributions from the pupils or other
teachers. Another broad principle which may be inferred from
what we have written is that the least elaborate method of
assessing is often the best — observing rather than testing, using
course work rather than formal examinations, and so on. For
one thing, the less elaborate the method, the less the danger
from incidental effects and time-wasting.

Assessments could be placed on a chart like this:

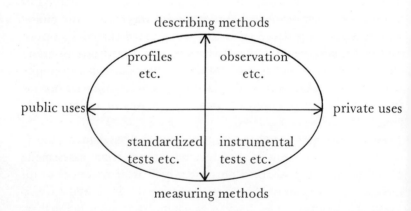

They are ranged on two spectra, one from public to private
uses, and one from measuring to describing methods. In general,
we think there is a danger that too many assessments will be

68

taken from the bottom left quadrant — measurements for public uses — and too few from the top right — observations for private uses. The bottom left assessments make us seem more accountable, so there is a tendency to veer towards them. It is a dangerous tendency because such assessments are often less appropriate for their purposes than are assessments in other quadrants, and because an emphasis on them may deflect attention from 'top right assessments' which would be more helpful. Sometimes, for instance, descriptive assessments, such as profiles, may be of more use to the public, and the observations on which they are based of more use to the teacher, than are standardized test results.

A better method than that used for assessing 'Lost in the Fog' would have been to type it out, perhaps with discreet corrections, for others to enjoy. That would have made its qualities clear and perhaps made clear the contribution of its correctness to the enjoyment of those qualities. (Encouragement to the writer to duplicate 'Drunken Pig' was an example of an appropriate method of assessment of this kind.) Even to ask other teachers or students to comment on 'Lost in the Fog' may have helped the teacher to see its meaning through its surface faults, and to make more apt comments on it. In the 'written examination alternative' (pp. 53—57) the collaborative scrutiny of recent course work and records of continuing conscious assessment was more appropriate for its predictive purpose than would have been the grading of scripts from a 'one-off' examination. In our reading case-histories, the teachers' assessments were appropriate for their purpose of assessing how pupils could cope with the literary and non-narrative texts they were meeting in the secondary school. Those assessments could have enlisted teachers of other subjects and provided precedents for continuing conscious assessing. The fact that Vivienne was allowed the attempt to read *My Childhood* was an appropriate assessment of her ability to cope with a full-length book, despite her weaknesses at reading. (That, of course, was a piece of luck: it would have been safer if a teacher who was both attentive and whom she trusted had judged that she could achieve this 'over-performance', rather than that a comparative stranger gave her the chance by accident — with a bigger risk of humiliating failure.) The letter accompanying the junior school report suggested that standardized tests and quantified judgments — 'marks' — had been the methods of production for the assessments which it reported. We think that continuing observation, perhaps aided by instrumental tests and checklists, would have been more appropriate methods for assessing primary children for any of the purposes we have listed, even public grading.

(c) Record and convey results in an appropriate form

We implied this guideline, a consequence of the first two, when we suggested parents and secondary teachers would receive more useful information, and be in less danger of being misled, if they were given descriptions of what primary children could do with language, rather than grades. For most purposes, a comparison of a pupil's performance with his previous performance is more helpful, to him, his parents, and his teachers, than a comparison with the performances of other pupils. When a comparison with others is needed, by an employer who wants to choose which of a pair will make the better clerk, for instance, that comparison will be better made from a 'profile' which describes in some detail particular performances, rather than from an overall grade or score. Teachers' records of assessments of pupils are best in a form which helps them to guide those pupils and plan their teaching of them. Their mark books should be more like notebooks than scoreboards. For instance, a record of *which* spelling mistakes a pupil makes (in 'Lost in the Fog', for instance) helps the teacher more than a record of *how many* spelling mistakes he makes, a record of what books (such as Gorky's *My Childhood*) a pupil has read, with what speed, difficulty, persistence, enjoyment, and so on, is more use in planning a pupil's reading programme than a reading age (there is no reason to think Vivienne's reading age would have 'improved' as a result of her successful reading of *My Childhood*). Our communications of assessments to our pupils need to be in forms which make them meaningful and helpful. It would be more help to the writer of 'Lost in the Fog' to tell him what that piece showed he had done well or badly than that he had earned 5/20. When assessment is evaluation ('well' or 'badly') it helps to define the criteria against which such an evaluation is being made. The writer of 'Lost in the Fog' had done well at shaping a story and at producing a sustained piece compared with previous work, but he had done badly, compared with expectations about his contemporaries, at making the story easy to read. This is true when evaluation is based on 'one-off' performances. We should make it clear to ourselves and to any other users that a 'Schonell Reading Age' is the result of one performance only at one test only of one reading sub-skill indicating to some extent only the efficiency with which that sub-skill will play its part in other readings. The junior school report should have made it clear what tests and markings its grades were based on and therefore to what extent they were accurate reflections of pupils' abilities compared to other pupils and what parts of 'English', 'Written', and 'Reading' they described. Parents are understandably worried about spelling, whilst junior teachers are justly proud of the creative writing which has burgeoned in many of their classes: a helpful form of primary report would allow for information being given explicitly about both these, and would discriminate between them.

(d)   Make your criteria explicit but flexible

Making criteria explicit is part of defining the purpose of assessment and couching records of assessment in appropriate forms. We hinted at some basic criteria, such as the effectiveness of language (which in some instances may outweigh correctness), or making meaning of what is read (rather than demonstrating an ability to analyse it in a literary or grammatical manner). But to apply criteria rigidly in assessment is inefficient teaching. Different uses of language call for the application of different criteria. For some uses, such as anecdotes, slang is appropriate, but for others, such as writing business letters, it is inappropriate. Silence can be good listening or poor talking. Quick reading can be efficient skimming or inefficient carelessness.

In approving Billy's talk, the teacher rightly applied the criteria of the interest of the class and the expertise in Billy's meaning, and he ignored elocution or restriction to personal material. In endorsing 'Drunken Pig', by allowing it to be copied, the teacher put its exemplary vividness above its unconventionalities of layout and punctuation. The teacher, taking an

71

overview of reading, looked for speed, persistence, and enjoyment, as well as for decoding skills.

Criteria should be applied flexibly as well as discriminatingly, or we may miss the individual growth points, or individual problems which idiosyncratic performances can signal. Even if 'Lost in the Fog' *had* been 'off the title' it would have been helpful to ignore that and to acknowledge its other qualities.

(e) Try to assess the language process

This is perhaps the hardest guideline to follow, and it is sometimes either impossible or impracticable to assess process except through product. Nevertheless, by attentive observation and the use of imagination we can infer what a pupil is doing with language. For instance, we can watch him reading, or talk to him about his reading when he pauses: this can provide more valid assessments of reading (though unquantifiable), than setting comprehension exercises and book reviews. It may also allow the teacher to note how a pupil moves his eyes, whether he points or moves his lips, and whether he self-corrects and uses clues. The two case-histories 'alternative to reading tests' illustrated this (pp. 45—48). Sometimes we can help children with writing as they write, and the observation this entails will help us to understand which technical mistakes are caused by carelessness, which by ignorance, and which by ambition, an understanding that *post facto* marking cannot always provide. It would be a pity if most marking (which may be the main kind of individual attention secondary pupils receive, and whose effectiveness decreases as the time increases between writing and marking) was not done in the pupil's presence. If we follow this guideline we will pay special attention to certain uses of language. For instance, the third year 'writing examination alternative' (pp. 53—57) took into account teachers' observations of the use of note-taking, which would be taken into account in the assessment. We may look at talk as a process of sorting out ideas (in group discussion, for instance) as well as polished performance, and reading as an assimilation of, and accommodation to, another person's experience, as well as a preliminary to answering written questions. A third consequence of following this guideline is that we will look at language products as evidence of processes. We will see, and assess, 'Lost in the Fog' as a re-creation of a personal experience, and an attempt to understand it rather than as a quarry of error; and we will see drafts of 'Drunken Pig' amongst other things as unprecedented examples of taking care and self-disciplining. One of our criticisms of the junior school report would be that it seems to treat reports, language, and children, as products. The report is 'the result of many hours marking', rather than a description of learning; language is assessed on test results and pieces of work, rather than as activity; and children are graded as if they were specimens, rather than recognized as changing individuals.

(f) Beware of the incidental effects of assessing

In criticizing some assessment procedures, we have referred to their incidental effects, which were not part of the original intention. One obvious unwelcome effect of assessing can be the waste of time involved in unnecessary, or unnecessarily formal, assessments. Sometimes the long-term effects of assessing may outweigh the short-term gains. Over-use of fast literary comprehension, such as that developed and assessed by reading laboratories, though it may boost speed, attentiveness and commitment in the short run, may teach a deleterious 'search and destroy' attitude to reading. Early over-emphasis on accuracy in speech, writing or reading can ultimately stunt language development by inhibiting fluent talk, ambitious writing, or quick reading. We think the effect of the teacher's low mark and criticism of 'Lost in the Fog' would be to discourage the writer from trying again. A third type of effect of assessment can be to limit teaching to the teaching of that which can be easily assessed. Oral work can become speech-making, reading can become recoding, and writing can become error-avoiding. That attitude can be conveyed to pupils — they can come to think that only examinations matter and that classwork is practice for examinations rather than a learning process. Finally, an obsession with quantifiable assessment can make the teacher less effective. A too careful categorization of pupils and materials may deprive pupils of such opportunities for language growth as Billy's talk, Vivienne's reading, or Michael's piece of writing. (We must qualify the last example, however: the teacher who taught Michael during the year after he wrote the piece thought the praise he had received for it led him to be complacent and hampered his development.) An effect of the report we cited might be to make pupils think that schoolwork is a show-jumping competition at which one aimed to eliminate rivals by clearing obstacles they hit.

(g) Make the best of a bad job

Ideally, in assessment, we should never use procedures which we would not use in our teaching. But what do we do when we have to assess for a purpose we do not share, by a method we think inappropriate or appropriate only for unhelpful purposes, by applying criteria we disagree with, or with what we think will be deleterious effects, and so on? Suppose our head teachers or LEAs require us to correct our pupils' regional pronunciations, or criticize us for allowing some spelling mistakes to pass uncorrected, or ask us to measure the reading ages of everyone in the school, or send the secondary school reading ages and grades, or set a formal timed examination to all the third-year pupils in our secondary school?

It is possible to mitigate the harm we anticipate from such procedures, and to salvage some incidental benefits from them, by following some of the guidelines set out above. For instance, a teacher obliged to test reading could choose to do so by using a test which involved some comprehension as well as word-recognition. Given no choice of test he could stress the limitations of the results when he presented them, and perhaps add to them some gratuitous information obtained by more valid assessments of reading. Collaboration can help. Teachers obliged to correct speech and spelling indiscriminately can explain to pupils and parents the social as well as linguistic criteria behind such pressures, and thus put into perspective the assessments heavily influenced by those criteria.

Teachers obliged to examine and grade can make clear (to everybody) the purposes and criteria behind the procedures, and in the process reap such incidental benefits as diagnosis of pupils' problems and training of inexperienced colleagues. Teachers obliged to pass on grades to others can make sure the grades are supported by evidence.

However, we should not like assessment of children's language to be regarded only in this pessimistic way — as a necessary evil. It can help the pupil and help the teacher to help the pupil. When there is an interest in, and an emphasis on, assessment, people are suggestible, and it is a good time to take the initiative and make positive proposals. In primary schools, class teachers and language consultants may find their advice and expertise both sought by, and welcome to busy headteachers. Secondary Heads of English may welcome suggestions that profile-recording, multiple-impression marking, reading checklists, or the use of course work in internal and external examinations be discussed and tried out in the school. External Examination Boards do invite teachers' comments and suggestions, and complain that they receive too few.

SECTION 2:
APPLYING THE GUIDELINES
TO THE FOUR ILLUSTRATIONS

(a) 'The day I tort the teachers'

How would guidelines like these affect our assessment of this story, which began both this book and our questions about assessment? What would we say to the writer, write on her book, write in our books, and so on?

First, one of the *purposes* of assessing the piece might be to find out if it was a good idea to encourage the pupils to write a 'reversed-role' story which engaged their interests and efforts. Another purpose might be to endorse the worthwhile nature of the activity for the writer. Another might be to judge what the writer most needed help with and how that help could best be given. This pupil seems to have a lively imagination, probably a good ear for speech, but difficulties in translating those gifts into writing. If we praise the exercise of the gifts, perhaps publicly, we might encourage care for such aspects of presentation as handwriting and consistent spelling.

So the appropriate *method* of assessing the story may be to praise it, to read it aloud, to type it with discreet corrections. Here we may enlist the writer's fellow-pupils ('What do you think of this?' 'Is it believable?' 'Did the "teacher" behave correctly?'

'What do you think of the ending?') or invite self-assessment and -correction ('Are there any improvements you'd like to make before you read it out?' or '. . . before I type it out?') Discussing and correcting the piece will best be done in the presence of the writer in a case like this. To correct all the mistakes or infelicities would almost certainly be counter-productive. Perhaps it would be unwise to correct anything at all outside the writer's presence, though to *praise* the change of 'teached' to 'tort' (sic) might be a discreet method of correction without failing to acknowledge a worthwhile self-correction. We need to judge our role as intended reader here. Are we being asked to share an experience as a friend, offer personal advice or reassurance, as a counsellor, or give technical advice as a master-craftsman? Only the teacher who has a personal relationship with the writer and reads the piece in the context of the pupil's other work can answer that.

In our mark book we might *record* an apparent concern for grading which we would want to discuss with the writer, an ability to shape a story, and an ability to reproduce speech accurately; but also carelessness with handwriting and inconsistency in spelling.

If we think this is an apprentice-piece of craftsmanship, our *criteria* will be technical ones. If we think it is a personal document, they will be personal ones. If we think the story is offered as an entertainment, our criteria will be perhaps the shape and its amusing effect as a story, qualities we would emphasize by having it read aloud or reproduced. That way we should emphasize the problems of presentation which would have to be solved or circumvented.

We should acknowledge that this story is a record of a shaping and a making of meaning — a *process* of understanding by helping the writer with what she seems to need, and by talking to her about what she was thinking and intending and wondering as she wrote.

The incidental *effects* we should avoid would be to inhibit further writing (by correcting all the spelling mistakes fiercely, for instance) or to mislead the writer about the criteria for judging stories (by damning the cliché-ending or disrespectful characterization of the Headmaster, for instance).

Finally, what if we should be too tired or overworked to attend to this story? What if we have insufficient time to discuss or mark it and all its fellows? How do we make the *best* of that? Some of the methods of assessment we have suggested are even more time-consuming than normal marking, and are only feasible if they are selective. If that is the case, and we do not have time to give the piece much attention, we should admit it to the pupil rather than disguise it by ticking or grading writing we have not read with care. We should explain to a class how their doing work is sometimes more important than our marking it, how we can welcome it by other means than routine scrutiny or thorough reading every time, how we sometimes assess by other means than writing on it, and how they and their friends can be the assessors of their own and of each others' work in certain ways. Sometimes we can conduct 'light sampling', so that on occasion all our pupils receive our proper attention to their work, but not every time.

(b) Administering a reading test

It is unlikely that a useful *purpose* would be served by measuring a reading age with a Schonell Graded Word Reading Test, for such scores are too coarse and imprecise for the week-by-week monitoring of progress which primary teachers require, although a list of such reading ages may give an appearance of monitoring. But if we were constrained to administer such tests for such purposes, we might make the *best* of the job by using it as an opportunity to talk with the readers or to do some diagnostic work (since an analysis of errors might reveal some phonic misunderstanding, for instance). It would at least give a chance for some detailed observation of the *process* of reading aloud, albeit of artificial material. But administering the test would not be the best *method* for the purpose of either diagnosis or observation, nor would the score obtained from the test be the appropriate *record* of what it revealed.

(c) Listening to a pupil reading from his reading scheme

For the *purposes* of diagnosing reading problems or observing reading strategies, and for matching pupils to print, listening to a pupil reading a real text is a better *method* than listening to him read a word-recognition test. It also provides an opportunity for discussion of the *meaning* of the text and therefore allows an assessment of comprehension and attitude to reading. As a result of the observation, a teacher could also *record* speed of reading, expressiveness of pronunciation, frequency and types of errors, degree of self-correction, use of context clues, and so on, as well as the name of the text, all better indicators of reading ability than a 'reading age'. Such a *record* will help the teacher plan future work with the pupil. But it is important that the record makes it clear that the information applies to reading aloud, and not necessarily to the fluent silent reading which may be more important to monitor at all but the earliest stages of reading. One method of acquiring information on silent reading and on reference skills would be to ask for the continuing conscious observation of any teachers who take the pupil.

Criteria which might be applied to the reading are fluency and expressiveness (signs of 'lower-order' reading skills and meaning-making, respectively). The observations are ones which get as near the *process* of reading as possible. If the text is a meaningful one, the pupil's enthusiasm for it, his relating of what he reads to what has gone before, his anticipation of what is to come, and his eagerness to find out how it ends, might be more apt criteria to apply to his reading than would be his word-by-word accuracy in sounding out words.

As long as elocution or word-by-word exactness are not compelled, and providing that the text is not worthless, the *effects* of a teacher listening to this reading may be to convey to the pupil a sense of the worth of careful, curious and responsive reading of meaningful texts. Making assessments only of the oral signs of reading, and especially of assessing by an over-scrupulous hearing of each class member read every day, merely produces young readers who 'bark at print', ignoring punctuation and meaning and stopping in mid-sentence at the end of every page.

If the text is one the teacher feels inappropriate, but is compelled to use, he may make the *best* of the job by practising some of the strategies suggested above, and frankly accepting the pupil's response to the text whatever this may be, thus teaching the truth that some texts are more worthwhile reading than others. A pupil has been known to answer a school-visitor's polite enquiry about the subject of his book with, 'It's not about anything, it's my *reading* book'.

(d)   Thinking about an examination and its result

Except in the cases of 'mock' examinations for GCE or CSE examinations, which provide practice for pupils and predictions for teachers, the *purposes* of internal examinations, such as the one in our illustration (pp. 7–9) are to provide information for reporting to parents and allotting children to courses. We have suggested that a teacher's knowledge and the pupil's course work provide more reliable evidence for such accounting, grading, and predicting, and that *methods* for examination should use that evidence by including the assessment of course work and continuing assessment. *Records* of such examinations are of most use to parents, employers, and teachers when they are descriptive and predictive, as are profiles and checklists. Such records make explicit the *criteria* against which assessments of success are made, whilst the methods of the examination allow a range of criteria to be deployed. Continuing assessment by teachers allows assessment to get nearer to the *process* of learning than does marking examination scripts, and thus the process has more predictive value. When an examination result has to be produced in terms of marks, those marks can be accompanied and qualified by notes and descriptions which make them more useful. When a formal examination has to be set, teachers can make the *best* of that constraint by making the work required in an examination as varied, natural, and similar to course work, as possible, and the assessment of it collaborative and personal.

Glossary

audience
the intended receiver (reader or hearer) of language.

checklist
a list of items of language behaviour, or other evidence, which helps to direct observation and ensure that it is thorough.

cloze procedure
a method of assessing or teaching reading by presenting texts in which words (a certain proportion or of a certain type) are deleted on a regular basis, and must be predicted from the context.

continuing assessment
assessment based on recurrent observations or tests over the period of a course rather than on a single occasion at the end of the course.

correctness
conformity to the accepted conventions of spelling, punctuation, grammar and layout of writing.

course work
the body of, or samples of, the work a pupil has done over the period of a course, on which an assessment can be made, rather than on the products of a single examination.

criterion-referenced test
test, the result of which tells whether or not a pupil can achieve certain performances rather than how his performance relates to those of other pupils.

decoding
turning print or sound into meaning.

diagnosis
deduction from language behaviours that a pupil has certain weaknesses, disabilities, misconceptions, or ignor-

	ances, or that he has certain strengths, abilities, understandings, or knowledge.
grading	allocating letters or figures to pupils' language performances (or putative abilities) so as to order them in relation to those of other children.
impression marking	grading work holistically as distinct from grading it according to a detailed marking scheme.
informal reading inventory	an assessment of a pupil's reading made by a teacher without standardized tests: it may use miscue analysis, notes on the pupil's comprehension, attitudes and reading record.
instrumental test	a test of whether or not a pupil can perform some specific task with language. A criterion-referenced test referred to a single pragmatic criterion.
miscue analysis	diagnosis based on annotations (with signs for omission, hesitations, mispronunciations, substitutions, self-corrections, and refusals) of a transcript of a reading text at the limit of a pupil's ability.
mode (of language)	reading, writing, speaking or listening.
mode 3 (of CSE)	syllabus set and assessment arranged by an individual school, or group of schools, with moderation by CSE Board.
morphology	the systematic way words change their forms according to their grammatical functions.
multiple impression marking	impression marking by a team of markers whose marks are averaged to arrive at a final grade. This method of marking helps to prevent a grade being awarded which might be distorted by individual carelessness and bias.
monitoring	assessing at regular intervals to com-

pare performances and infer progress.

normal distribution a certain distribution which is bell-shaped in its graphical presentation. It has a precise mathematical formulation and approximates to many naturally occurring distributions e.g. height of adults.

norm-referenced test a test of which the result gives a comparison between the performance of the tested pupil and the average performances at the test by equivalent pupils: for instance, a reading age is the age of pupils who, on average, achieve the same score as the pupil being tested.

profiles a description of a pupil's language performances categorized according to certain types of observation, behaviour, test result, or ability.

readability the ease with which words (as distinct from print) can be read; it is calculated by various formulae, most of which assume it to be inversely related to sentence length and frequency of long words, and it is expressed as an index which indicates the age at which the average pupil can be expected to comprehend the text to which it refers.

recoding changing print into sound or vice versa.

reliability the correlation between a score on a test or assessment on one occasion and the score on the same test or assessment by an equivalent pupil on another occasion, or between one marker's score and another's of the same material.

response a pupil's reaction to a text or other

	utterance: it includes, but is not confined to, comprehension.
screening	using an assessment procedure to separate some pupils from others for special treatment.
self-assessment	an assessment by a pupil of his own performance or abilities.
validity	the degree to which a test measures what it purports to measure.
withdrawal	removal of a pupil from lessons for special remedial help on his own or in a small group.

Bibliography

This is a short list of books with valuable statements or implications about aspects of the assessment of children's language. It includes all the books referred to in the text, plus a few more.

General

HMSO (1975) *A language for Life*: The Bullock Report

NATE (1977) *English in Education*: The Assessment of English Vol. 11 No. 2

DIXON (1975) *Growth Through English* 3rd Edition OUP for NATE

WILKINSON (1978) 'Criteria of Language Development' in *Educational Review* Vol. 30 No. 1. 1978

On listening

WILKINSON, STRATTA and DUDLEY (1974) *The Quality of Listening* Macmillan for Schools Council

On Talk

TOUGH (1976) *Listening to Children Talking* Ward Lock Educational for Schools Council

On Reading

General

MELNIK and MERRITT (1972a) *The Reading Curriculum* ULP for Open University

MELNIK and MERRITT (1972b) *Reading Today and Tomorrow* ULP for Open University

STRANG, McCULLOUGH and TRAXLER (1967) *The Improvement of Reading*: 4th edition McGraw Hill

LONGLEY (ed) 1977 *Reading After Ten* BBC

Learning to Read

KOHL (1974) *Reading, How to* Penguin

LONGLEY (ed) (1976) *Teaching Young Readers* BBC
SMITH (1973) *Psycholinguistics and Reading* Holt, Rinehart,
  Winston

Comprehension and Response
D'ARCY (1973) *Reading for Meaning* Vol. II Hutchinson for
  Schools Council
DIXON, BARNES and BROWN (1977) *Developing Active Com-
  prehension*, Schools Council English 16–19 Project, Bretton
  Hall College, W. Yorks.

Testing
PUMFREY (1976) *Reading Tests and Assessment Techniques*
  Hodder and Stoughton for UKRA

Readability
GILLILAND (1972) *Readability* Hodder and Stoughton for
  UKRA

On Writing

General
BRITTON, MARTIN, ROSEN, McLEOD and BURGESS
  (1975) *The Development of Writing Abilities 11–18* Macmillan
HARPIN (1976) *The Second R* Unwin
MARTIN et al (1976) *Writing and Learning across the Curriculum* Ward Lock Educational for Schools Council
MOFFETT (1968) *Teaching the Universe of Discourse* Hough-
  ton Mifflin

On Marking
ADAMS and PEARCE (1974) *Every English Teacher* OUP
BRITTON, MARTIN and ROSEN (1966) *Multiple Impression
  Marking of English Compositions* Schools Council Exam-
  inations Bulletin No. 2 HMSO
STRATTA (1973) 'Some Consideration When Marking' in
  Patterns of Language Heinemann

WADE (1978) 'Responses to Written Work: the possibilities of utilizing pupils' perceptions' in *Educational Review: The Learner's Viewpoint* Vol. 30 No. 2 1978

On Spelling
TORBE (1977) *Teaching Spelling* Ward Lock Educational

On Examinations
PEARCE (1974) in Forsyth and Pearce: *Language: Classrooms and Examinations* Longman for Schools Council

Teaching Spelling
Mike Torbe

Just how important is correct spelling? Important enough for most teachers and many parents to be anxious about it. Some children do seem to be able to spell without ever being taught, but most need help to become efficient spellers; and teachers and parents have always known how difficult it is to find out what help to give, and how best to give it.

Teaching Spelling tries to answer the kinds of question often asked about the teaching of spelling. It describes, clearly, practically and methodically, a way in which the reader can identify the underlying causes of failure to spell, and also how to set about improving spelling. There is advice on making corrections, on common mistakes and how to analyse errors, as well as suggestion for games and teaching ideas. Teachers with pupils of all ages who find spelling difficult will welcome this manual, and find it an invaluable aid.

Mike Torbe is Curriculum Development Officer for Coventry. He has written several books on aspects of language teaching and has taught in secondary and primary schools and a College of Education.

Revised edition
ISBN 0 7062 3851 6 £1.25 net UK only

Language across the Curriculum
Guidelines for Schools

Mike Torbe, for the National Association for the Teaching of English

Following the Bullock Report's recommendation that schools 'should develop a policy for language across the curriculum', many schools have become interested in language across the curriculum but have found beginning work on a language policy difficult. This practical document, produced by HMIs, advisers, headteachers and people working in schools and universities, will help schools to develop their own language policy.

38pp. 0 7062 3619 X **80p** net (pb)